Living After

Living After

Stories of Moral Injury Among Disaster Survivors

G. C. SMITH

RESOURCE *Publications* • Eugene, Oregon

LIVING AFTER
Stories of Moral Injury Among Disaster Survivors

Resource Publications
An Imprint of Wipf and Stock Publishers
199 W. 8th Ave., Suite 3
Eugene, OR 97401

www.wipfandstock.com

PAPERBACK ISBN: 979-8-3852-8590-7
HARDCOVER ISBN: 979-8-3852-8591-4
EBOOK ISBN: 979-8-3852-8592-1

VERSION NUMBER 05/14/26

This book is a work of narrative reflection. While it draws on real experiences and themes common to disaster response and recovery, all personal stories have been adapted, anonymized, or composited to protect the privacy and dignity of individuals. Any resemblance to specific persons, living or deceased, is coincidental.

The author acknowledges the profound weight carried by disaster survivors and offers this work as a contribution to ongoing conversations about moral injury, healing, and human dignity.

For those who lived through what could not be made whole
and continued.

For those who carried what remained
when nothing resolved.

For those whose decisions were shaped by limits
no one should be asked to bear.

For those who remember not only what was lost,
but what could not be saved.

For those who speak, and for those who cannot.

For those who stay present
even when presence does not change the outcome.

And for those who live after—
not restored, not completed,
but still here.

Contents

Introduction

Living After

Disasters end.

This is how they are recorded, how they are measured, how they are spoken about when the language turns toward order again. The storm passes. The water recedes. The fire is contained. The ground stops moving. The official markers are clear enough to hold in a report: time of impact, duration, number affected, number displaced, number dead. There is a point at which the event is said to be over, and from that point forward, everything that follows is named differently—recovery, rebuilding, return.

But for those who live through disaster, the ending does not arrive in that way.

It does not arrive as a clean line between what happened and what comes next. It does not divide the world into before and after with the clarity that the language suggests. Instead, something remains—not only in memory, not only in loss, but in the way the world itself is held. What was once assumed about safety, about responsibility, about what can be relied upon, no longer holds in the same way. The structure of meaning shifts, sometimes suddenly, sometimes slowly, but once it has shifted, it does not return to its previous form.

This book attends to that space.

Not to the disaster as an event, but to what continues after it. Not to the immediate experience of survival, but to the moral life that follows survival—the questions that do not resolve, the moments that do not settle, the weight that does not lift when the visible work of response and recovery has been completed.

In After the Disaster: Moral Injury, Dignity, and the Lives of Survivors, I explored the framework for understanding this reality. Moral injury, in that work, is not limited to those who act under pressure, though it includes them. It extends also to those who endure, who witness, who survive. It names the rupture that occurs when what a person has lived through cannot be reconciled with what they believe about themselves, about others, or about the world. It is not only the question of what happened, but of what it means that it happened—and what it means that one continues to live in its aftermath.

This book does not explain that framework.

It inhabits it.

The stories that follow are not case studies, not illustrations, not examples designed to clarify a concept. They are narrative accounts of survivors whose lives have been altered in ways that are not resolved by time, by distance, or by the restoration of external conditions. Homes may be rebuilt. Communities may return. Systems may function again. But the moral landscape within which a person lives has shifted, and that shift remains.

Each story centers on a moment.

Not always the most dramatic moment, not always the most visible, but the one in which something irreversible occurred. A decision that could not be undone. A recognition that could not be set aside. A failure that cannot be corrected. A survival that cannot be explained in a way that satisfies the one who lives with it. These moments are often small in outward appearance, but they carry a weight that extends far beyond the time in which they occurred. They become reference points, returned to again and again, not because the person chooses to return, but because the moment itself has not finished with them.

These are not stories of resilience in the way that term is often used. They do not move toward restoration or resolution. They do not offer closure. They do not attempt to reconcile what has happened into a form that can be accepted and set aside. Instead, they remain where they are, attentive to the fact that for many survivors, the work is not to move on, but to continue living in the presence of what cannot be resolved.

This is where dignity becomes essential.

Dignity, in this context, is not a quality that emerges after healing. It is not dependent on recovery or on the restoration of coherence. It is present in the act of continuing to live, even when what one lives with cannot be made sense of. It is present in the refusal—whether conscious or not—to reduce one's experience to something smaller than it is, to explain it away, to deny its weight. It is present in the quiet, often unseen ways in which a person holds together a life that has been altered in ways that cannot be reversed.

The survivors in these stories are not passive. Even when they could not act in the moment, even when they were overcome by forces beyond their control, they remain morally engaged with what has occurred. They ask questions that do not have answers. They revisit decisions that cannot be changed. They live with the awareness that something was required, or might have been required, and that the relationship between what was possible and what was done cannot be easily resolved.

This is the terrain of moral injury among survivors.

It is quieter than the terrain of response. It does not carry the same urgency. It does not demand immediate action. But it is no less significant. It unfolds over time, often in private, often without language that adequately captures it. It appears in memory, in relationships, in the way a person inhabits space, in what they can and cannot return to, in what they carry forward even when everything else suggests that the disaster has ended.

These stories are offered without resolution.

They do not seek to fix what cannot be fixed. They do not attempt to bring comfort where comfort would diminish the truth of what is being carried. They remain with the survivors as they are—with the questions, with the weight, with the ongoing work of living after.

To read them is not to understand them fully.

It is to remain with them.

And perhaps, in remaining, to recognize something of what it means to live when the disaster is over—and not over at all.

PART I

The Moment That Divides

STORY 1

The One Who Was Chosen

BEFORE THE WATER CAME, the house held in the way houses are expected to hold, not because it had been tested or proven under pressure, but because it existed within a pattern that had never required examination. The walls stood where they had always stood, the doors opened and closed with the same resistance they had the day they were installed, and the windows carried light in the morning and reflected it back in the evening without interruption. There was no reason to question any of it. The river remained at a distance that had always felt sufficient, the ground between house and water remained stable, and the boundary between what belonged to the river and what belonged to those who lived beside it had never needed to be named in order to be trusted.

The morning unfolded within that structure without interruption. The kitchen light came on before the sun had fully reached the windows, and the coffee maker filled the room with a familiar sound that marked the beginning of the day more reliably than any clock. The older child sat at the table, still waking, one hand resting around a glass that had not yet been lifted, while the younger moved between rooms carrying objects from one place to another without purpose beyond motion. The rhythm of the house did not require attention to sustain it; it continued because it had always continued.

There were small variations that morning, though none presented themselves as warnings. The air carried a density that did not align with any season she could identify, and the light entering through the windows seemed to settle more slowly than usual, as if passing through something not visible. It was not darker, and it was not dimmed, but it lacked the clarity it had carried the day before. The difference did not announce itself as change. It existed as a slight delay, a hesitation in what should have been immediate, and for a time it remained within the range of what could be ignored.

The older child paused once at the table, his hand still around the glass, his attention directed beyond the room toward something that had not yet formed into sound. He did not speak or ask a question. After a moment, he resumed eating, the interruption closing without explanation. The younger continued moving between spaces, placing objects down and retrieving others, his attention guided by nothing that required completion. The house absorbed all of it without resistance.

She poured coffee and remained at the counter longer than necessary, her hand resting against the surface, her body still while her attention extended outward. She did not know what she was listening for, only that something had not yet arrived. The absence did not have a name. It existed as a delay, a space where something familiar had failed to present itself at the expected time.

She did not think of the river as something capable of behaving differently than it had before. It had a place, a direction, and a history measured in seasons rather than in hours. When it rose, it did so gradually. When it receded, it left behind evidence but not disruption. The possibility that it could leave its banks not as overflow but as force did not exist within her understanding of the world. This was not denial. It was structure. The world held because it had always held.

The first indication came as absence. The usual sound of traffic beyond the tree line did not arrive at the expected time. The road that ran parallel to the river carried a steady movement of vehicles each morning, a pattern so consistent it had become background, noticed only when it was missing. She stood at the sink, her hand still resting against the counter, listening not yet for meaning but for confirmation. When the sound did not return, the absence extended beyond what could be dismissed as variation.

She waited.

The delay did not resolve.

She wiped her hands and moved to the window, looking toward the road. The view was partially obscured by trees, but enough remained visible to confirm what she already sensed. There was no movement, no vehicles, and no sound. The space where motion should have been remained empty in a way that did not align with any ordinary interruption. She did not immediately think of the river. She thought of an accident, of road work, of something contained within a system that would make sense once explained. The world still held. It had not yet shifted.

The second absence altered that assumption. The neighbor's dog, which barked at everything and nothing, remained quiet, not briefly but in a sustained absence that did not align with its nature. The quiet extended beyond the road and into the spaces between houses that normally carried sound even when nothing specific could be identified. She listened again, this time with intention, and found that what remained was not silence but the absence of interruption.

She turned back into the room and told the children to finish their breakfast, her voice even enough that neither of them looked up. There was no reason for them to yet. She moved to the back door, opened it, and stepped into air that felt denser than it should have, carrying a weight that did not belong to the morning. It did not press against her or resist her. It simply occupied the space in a way that required acknowledgment without offering explanation.

The yard appeared unchanged at first glance. The ground held its shape. The tree line remained where it had always been. The structures that defined the space still existed in their expected positions. Nothing had been displaced.

Then she saw it.

Not the river itself, but the distance between ground and trees. It had shortened. Not dramatically and not in a way that would draw attention from someone unfamiliar with that space, but enough that she could not dismiss it. She had walked that ground too many times not to know its measure. What had existed there before no longer existed in the same way.

She stepped onto the porch, not to investigate but to confirm. The boards creaked under her weight as they always did, and the railing remained firm beneath her hand. The structure of the house was unchanged. The difference lay beyond it. The line that had once marked the boundary between yard and river had shifted forward, reducing the space between them in a way that did not announce itself through force but through quiet occupation.

She remained there longer than necessary, watching not for sudden movement but for continuation. The water did not rush or surge. It advanced steadily, occupying space that had not belonged to it before. It did not retreat or pause. It continued.

Recognition formed gradually, not as alarm but as alignment between what she saw and what she could no longer deny. The distance between what had been safe and what was no longer safe shortened in increments too small to track moment by moment and too consistent to ignore once seen.

When she turned back into the house, her movement had changed. It did not become hurried, but it no longer belonged to the rhythm that had defined the morning. She told the children to get their shoes, the words carrying direction rather than explanation. When the older child asked where they were going, she repeated the instruction instead of answering. The younger did not ask. He moved immediately, responding to the shift in her voice.

She moved through the space quickly but without searching, taking only what was immediately available. Keys. Phone. Jacket. The act of gathering did not expand into decision. It remained within the limits of what could be carried without delay.

When she returned to the doorway, the water had moved again.

The difference was no longer subtle.

It had entered the yard.

The distance between porch and ground had closed.

She told them to come, and they moved with her.

By the time she stepped off the porch and into the yard, the ground no longer responded in the way it always had. It did not give way, but it no longer held with the same certainty, and the difference required attention even as she moved quickly across it. Each step pressed slightly into the surface, the soil yielding just enough to alter balance without collapsing entirely. The water had not yet reached the porch, but it had entered the yard in a way that removed any remaining distance between observation and involvement. What had been seen from the threshold now had to be crossed.

The children moved with her without instruction, their proximity tightening in response to the change in her movement. The older child stayed close enough to reach without extending, his attention divided between her and the space behind them, while the younger followed at her side, his motion less directed but drawn toward her with increasing consistency. Neither of them spoke. The absence of explanation did not yet require filling. It remained contained within the pace she set.

The truck stood where it always had, positioned in the drive at an angle that allowed for immediate departure under ordinary conditions. Nothing about it had changed. It remained intact, accessible, and within reach. She moved toward it with the same expectation that had governed every previous departure, her body following a sequence that had never failed to produce movement. The distance between the house and the vehicle closed quickly, though the ground beneath her feet required more attention than before.

She opened the back door and directed the older child to move across the seat, her hand guiding him forward without pause. The younger began to cry, not loudly, but with the uneven breath that precedes it, the sound rising from disruption rather than understanding. She lifted him under the arms and placed him onto the seat beside his brother, steadying him as his foot slipped briefly before finding its place. The contact did not linger. It moved quickly from one action to the next, each step in the sequence following the last without interruption.

She closed the door and moved around the truck, already reaching for the key as she entered the driver's side. The motion was continuous and unbroken by hesitation. For a moment, the system held. The engine turned, the vehicle responded, and the familiar alignment between action and result remained intact. She shifted into reverse and pressed the accelerator, expecting the immediate movement that had always followed.

The engine answered.

The ground did not.

The truck rocked slightly, then settled back into place, the tires spinning against a surface that absorbed the force without translating it into motion. She pressed harder, shifting into drive and attempting forward movement, but the result did not change. The vehicle remained where it was, its response limited to sound and vibration, neither of which produced the outcome required.

She remained seated for a fraction longer than necessary, her hands still on the wheel, her body waiting for a correction that did not come. The expectation that effort would produce movement did not resolve. It remained unmet, and in that failure the structure that had governed the situation shifted.

The children's voices filled the space, their crying no longer contained but immediate, requiring response even as she could not yet provide one that would restore the conditions they expected. She turned off the engine, not as a decision but as a response to the sound of effort that no longer produced result. The silence that followed revealed everything else—the water pressing against the underside of the truck, the uneven breathing of the younger child, and the older child speaking in a way that did not yet reach her as meaning.

She told them they were getting out.

The older child asked why, and she repeated the instruction rather than explaining it. The words did not function as explanation. They functioned as direction, and the direction was sufficient.

When she opened the door and stepped down, the water had risen further, now moving around her legs with a steady, directional force. It was no longer contained within the yard as a presence. It had become a condition through which movement had to occur. She moved to the back door and opened it, lifting the younger child first, his arms wrapping around her neck without instruction, his body responding to the change in position before understanding it.

The older child climbed out behind him, reaching for her as he found his footing. She told him to hold on, and he did, his hand closing around her sleeve before shifting to her arm as the fabric lost its ability to hold tension under the water. The contact adjusted without instruction, his grip seeking a position that would remain secure.

She left everything else behind. The bag remained in the front seat. The keys remained in the ignition. The house stood behind them with the door still open. None of it belonged to what came next.

She turned toward the road, which remained in her mind as direction rather than certainty, the only path that suggested distance from what was advancing. The water reached her calves before they had crossed half the yard, and the slope that had always drained water now gathered it, pulling it into the space she needed to cross. The ground beneath her feet no longer provided consistent resistance, and each step required adjustment that did not carry forward into the next.

The older child stumbled once, then again, his grip tightening each time as his footing failed to hold. He said that he was trying, his voice breaking between words, and she told him that she knew, the exchange occurring within movement that did not pause for either of them. The younger child pressed into her shoulder, his arms tightening around her neck, his weight shifting with each step she took.

They reached the drive, where the water deepened further and the current gathered enough force to alter their balance with each movement. Her foot did not find ground immediately as she stepped forward.

She shifted her weight, caught herself, and in that shift felt the older child lose his footing completely.

She caught him by the wrist.

The motion was immediate and unconsidered, her hand closing around him as his body moved outward, the current pulling him away from her center. The contact between them changed in that instant. It was no longer guidance. It was anchoring.

Now she held one in her arms and one in her hand.

The water continued to rise.

She adjusted her stance, widening her footing in an attempt to create stability where none existed, but the ground beneath her did not respond consistently. What held under one step failed under the next, and the effort required to maintain balance increased with each movement forward. The younger child's weight pressed downward and inward at the same time, his grip tightening around her neck, pulling her slightly off center each time she attempted to correct.

The older child's arm extended further from her body as the current moved against him, increasing the distance between where she could stabilize herself and where he was positioned. She tightened her grip on his wrist, feeling the structure beneath the skin, anchoring not just his movement but the connection itself, her hand adjusting to compensate for the loss of friction that had once allowed contact to hold without force.

She stepped again, and the ground gave more than it had before, her foot sliding just enough to require immediate correction. The shift altered the angle between them, and his body moved outward again, his footing no longer aligned with hers. She pulled him back toward her, but the movement did not restore their earlier position. It created a new one, less stable than the last.

The current did not increase or change direction. It remained steady, and within that steadiness the limits of what she could maintain became clearer. Each correction required more effort than the one before, and each produced less stability.

She tried again, adjusting the younger child higher against her shoulder to bring his weight closer to her center, but the motion shifted her balance just enough for the current to take advantage of it. Her foot slipped again, and in that slip the older child's body moved further outward, the distance widening beyond what could be recovered through a single movement.

She tightened her grip again, her fingers pressing into a position that held only because she forced it to hold. The contact no longer rested in place. It required constant maintenance, constant correction, and continuous effort that did not accumulate into stability.

She did not stop moving, because stopping would not restore anything. She continued forward in increments that no longer resembled walking but became a sequence of controlled recoveries, each step an attempt to remain upright while holding two positions that could not both be secured.

The moment did not break.

It narrowed.

The water continued to move around them with steady force, and that steadiness, more than any surge or visible violence, altered what remained possible. Nothing in it suggested interruption. It did not rise dramatically from one second to the next, and it did not strike with enough suddenness to be named as impact. It persisted, pressing against her legs, against the child in her arms, and against the child in her hand, and within that persistence the limits of what her body could maintain became clearer than any thought she might have formed.

She adjusted her footing again, widening her stance as far as the ground beneath her would allow, trying to create stability through position rather than movement. The attempt held only briefly. One foot found resistance and the other did not, and the unevenness beneath her forced another correction before the last one had completed. The younger child's weight pressed downward and inward at the same time, his body clinging to her not in coordination with her motion but in resistance to it, each tightening of his grip altering her center of balance by a degree too small to name and too consequential to ignore.

The older child's body remained angled outward from her, his footing lost and partially regained in irregular succession as the current moved against him. His free arm lifted and lowered without intention, searching not for direction but for balance. His hand on her wrist shifted each time the water pulled, the contact no longer something that could be maintained through certainty but something that had to be remade continuously through force.

She tightened her grip and pulled him closer. For a moment, the distance narrowed and his shoulder aligned more directly with her. For a moment, it seemed possible that the position could be restored. Then the ground beneath her right foot yielded more than it had before, not collapsing entirely but giving enough to tilt her body off center. The correction required to recover from that shift pulled against the weight of the younger child and the current moving across the older one, and in that instant the three of them no longer formed a position that could be carried forward without loss.

"Stay up," she said, and the words came sharper than she intended, not because she believed he could comply by will alone, but because the command was the only form language still held in a moment that had already moved beyond it.

"I am trying," he said again.

This time the words landed differently. They did not function as reassurance or response. They stood as statement, as fact, and she believed him completely. That recognition did not change anything. It clarified it.

She took another step. Her foot slid, and the older child's arm jerked hard against her grip. The younger child tightened around her neck with enough force to pull her backward at the shoulders even as the current pressed forward against her legs. Her body responded by trying to divide itself into two separate acts of holding, and in doing so it reached the point where neither could be sustained in full.

Forward movement ceased, not as a decision but because it no longer existed in a form she could take. The road remained ahead, but the relation between where she stood and where she needed to be had changed. Distance was no longer measured in yards. It was measured in what could be held across the next shift of balance, the next pull of current, the next failure of ground.

The older child slipped lower, not fully into the water but enough to change the angle between them, shifting the strain on her arm from outward pull to downward drag. She tightened again, her fingers pressing into his wrist with enough force that she would later remember the exact structure beneath the skin, but the contact had already altered. It no longer secured him in place. It only delayed his movement away from her.

She adjusted the younger child higher against her shoulder, trying to bring his weight closer to her center, trying to reduce the distance between effort and balance. The motion required only a small shift, but within the conditions that held them it was enough. Her torso turned slightly, her footing altered, and the older child's body moved outward again as the current followed the angle it had been given.

She pulled him back, and for an instant she felt the full return of his weight, transferred directly through her arm and shoulder rather than distributed through the water. It was more than she could hold and less than she could release. The younger child responded to the same movement by tightening further, his breath breaking against her neck in a sharp, uneven burst that registered physically before it registered as sound.

Everything narrowed.

There was no longer house, yard, road, or river. There was only force, weight, grip, ground, and the diminishing interval in which all of it could remain joined.

She did not think in terms of choosing. The word had no place in what was happening. There was no weighing of one against the other, no internal calculation, no moment in which alternatives were considered. What existed instead was a convergence of limits. Her body had reached the point at which it could not maintain both holds against the conditions pressing through them, and the effort to do so no longer preserved anything. It only extended the interval before loss completed itself.

She knew this before she could have said it. The knowledge registered first in the strain of her arm, in the exact sensation of her grip shifting from secure to temporary, in the way the muscles began to tremble, not from weakness alone, but from the effort of holding against something that did not lessen. It registered in the redistribution of weight that pulled her away from the child she held by the wrist and toward the one she carried.

She pulled once more with everything she had.

For less than a second, he came closer, and in that brief alignment the world clarified. His face came fully into view, not through motion but through stillness. His mouth was open, though she could not hear what he might have been saying. His eyes were fixed on her, not only in fear but in recognition, as if her presence remained more stable than anything else around them.

Her grip failed.

Not because she opened her hand.

Not because she released him.

Because the position required to hold him no longer existed.

His hand moved across hers. The contact shifted from grip to sliding pressure. His fingers caught briefly against her palm, then slipped free and did not catch again.

The separation was immediate and complete. One moment there was contact. The next there was not.

He moved away at once, carried sideways by the current that had already been holding him in that direction. She saw him. That remained with absolute clarity. His head stayed above the water for an instant longer. His arms moved without coordination. The distance between them increased before it could be measured.

She did not move toward him.

She could not.

Her body had already committed fully to stabilizing the child in her arms, and that act consumed everything that remained available to her. The current continued without interruption. The ground beneath her did not become more reliable. Nothing adjusted in response to what had just occurred.

She saw him.

That remained.

The moment did not slow or widen. It completed itself, and the world continued.

For an instant longer, her hand retained the shape of its hold. Her fingers remained closed around the space his wrist had occupied, the memory of contact persisting beyond the contact itself. She felt the absence before she named it, the position of her hand still organized around what was no longer there.

Then the younger child shifted in her arms, his weight pulling her off center again, and the next act of holding began.

She adjusted, found her footing as best she could, and took another step, then another. Forward movement resumed, not because the path had cleared or because what had been lost could be set aside, but because stopping would not return it. The road remained ahead. The child in her arms remained within reach. The current pressed against her legs.

Everything that could not be changed had already changed.

And still she moved.

She reached the road without registering the sequence of steps that carried her there. The movement from water to ground remained part of the same effort until it met a surface firm enough to hold her weight without shifting. The change in footing registered as difference rather than relief, one condition replaced by another without resolving what had already taken place.

Hands reached for her as soon as she entered the space where others had gathered. They established contact quickly, guiding her without force in a direction she did not need to choose. Someone took the child from her arms, and the removal of his weight registered as alteration, her body adjusting to the absence of what it had been compensating for. She did not resist or assist. It occurred around her.

Voices followed in patterns that suggested structure. She heard them, but the words did not settle into meaning. They passed through without attaching.

"He is okay," someone said.

She saw him.

That registered.

They asked where the other child was.

She turned toward the water.

"He was right there," she said.

The words located.

They did not describe.

They moved her. They seated her. They asked again. She answered the same way.

"He was right there."

The space had already changed.

Distance increased.

Nothing else did.

Time continued.

The language held.

"The water came up too fast."

"I was trying to get them out."

"He slipped."

The account remained.

Her hands rested in her lap, her fingers still curved.

She held one.

The other had not remained.

Days passed.

The house resumed its form.

The child remained near.

Her hand closed sometimes.

Then opened.

Around nothing.

At night, she stood in the doorway.

Watching.

Not for movement.

For presence.

Years passed.
From the outside, her life resumed.
From the inside, it did not.
When people asked what had happened, she answered.
“I held them.”
It was enough.
It was not the whole.
She continued.
That is what remained.

STORY 2

The Door That Closed

Before the storm, the doors in the house worked without drawing attention to themselves. They opened when pushed, closed when released, and held their position without drifting or resisting. Their hinges carried weight without sound. Their frames met cleanly. They marked boundaries between rooms in a way that required no thought, separating one space from another while allowing the house to function as a whole. The front door sealed firmly against the outside, and the interior doors moved easily enough that they could be left partially open without shifting on their own.

The house stood in a neighborhood where the spacing between homes had been measured carefully, each one set back from the street and from the others in a pattern that allowed for distance without isolation. The street curved slightly, enough to slow traffic but not enough to obscure what lay ahead, and the houses followed that curve in a line that felt ordered without being identical. Trees had been planted at intervals years earlier and had since grown beyond their original plan, their branches extending over the street in uneven arcs that filtered the light and moved with the wind without blocking it.

Inside, the morning followed its usual sequence. The kitchen light came on before the sun reached the windows, and the coffeemaker began its cycle, the sound steady and predictable. He moved through the routine without pausing to consider it, each step connected to the next in a way that no longer required decision. The hallway door remained partially open, as it always did, allowing sound to travel from the bedrooms into the kitchen without interruption.

His daughter came down first. Her steps were even, her movement familiar, and she passed through the doorway without touching it, leaving it in the same position it had held before she entered the room. She sat at the table and reached for the glass that had been set there the night before, lifting it slightly before setting it back down again, the motion incomplete but unremarkable.

He poured coffee and remained at the counter a moment longer than necessary, his hand resting against the surface. The house held its usual sounds—the quiet hum of appliances, the faint movement of air through vents, the subtle shifting of structure as temperature changed. Nothing in it demanded attention. And yet there was a slight irregularity within it, something that did not separate itself fully from the background but did not settle into it either, a small misalignment that could not be named.

Outside, the wind moved through the trees without yet becoming distinct. Branches shifted. Leaves turned. The air carried pressure, but not enough to register as change. It remained within what could be ignored, part of the ordinary variation of the morning.

The radio sat on the counter, its volume low. A voice spoke steadily, delivering information in a tone that suggested continuity rather than urgency. The words entered the room without altering it. He did not turn toward it.

His daughter asked whether school would still be open. Her voice carried the question without concern, as if asking for confirmation rather than expecting change. He answered that it would, because it always had, because the conditions that would close it had not yet entered into what he understood as possible. The answer settled easily between them.

The hallway door shifted slightly.

Not enough to close. Not enough to draw attention.

But enough to change position.

He noticed it without turning, registering the movement in the same way he had registered the earlier irregularity, as something that existed without requiring response. The house adjusted to small changes all the time. Air moved. Pressure shifted. Doors responded. Nothing in that movement required interpretation.

He moved toward the window and looked out at the street. The trees had begun to move more noticeably now, their branches bending with a direction that had not been present earlier. Leaves lifted and turned, exposing their undersides in flashes that caught the light differently. The sky held its color, but the light beneath it had flattened slightly, as if depth had been reduced without being removed.

A car passed along the street more slowly than usual, its motion deliberate. He watched it move through the curve and out of sight, the sound of its engine carrying longer than expected before fading.

Behind him, the hallway door moved again.

This time it closed.

The sound was quiet, but complete. The latch met the frame, and the space between open and closed disappeared.

He turned.

The door remained still.

He stood where he was for a moment, aware that no one had touched it, that it had moved without intention, and that the house around it had not changed in any visible way. The sounds continued. The light remained. The morning did not stop.

But something no longer aligned.

He walked toward the door, his movement steady, unchanged from the rest of the morning. When he reached it, he placed his hand on the handle and turned it. The latch disengaged cleanly, the mechanism working as it always had.

He pushed.

The door moved slightly.

Then stopped.

He waited, his hand still on the handle, as if the resistance might release on its own.

It did not.

He pushed again, applying more pressure, aligning his weight behind the motion. The door shifted a fraction further, then held.

The obstruction was not in the door.

It was beyond it.

He called her name.

No answer came.

—

He did not release the handle right away. His hand remained on it, holding the latch open as if the delay between movement and response might resolve if he gave it time. The mechanism had worked. He could feel that clearly. The failure did not lie in the door itself. It lay somewhere on the other side of it, in a space he could not yet see.

He pushed again, more firmly this time, bringing his shoulder behind the motion so that the force carried through his body instead of just his arm. The door moved slightly, enough to confirm that it was not fixed in place, but it did not open far enough to allow passage. Whatever pressed against it held with weight, not tension. It did not give. It absorbed the effort and remained.

He called her name again, louder now, directing the sound through the narrow gap that had opened and into the space beyond. The wind outside had begun to press more noticeably against the house, the sound of it no longer blending into the background. It moved in uneven intervals, rising and falling, striking the structure in a way that carried through the walls and into the hallway.

No answer came.

He released the handle and stepped back half a pace, not retreating, just creating space to change how he approached it. He placed his palm flat against the door and pressed, feeling for any difference across its surface, any place where the resistance might be less complete. There was none. The pressure held evenly from top to bottom, as if something large and solid had settled against it.

He set his shoulder against the wood and pushed again. The frame flexed slightly under the effort, a small give that belonged to the structure itself, not to whatever blocked it. The door shifted a fraction and returned, the resistance unchanged.

He called her name again.

Still nothing.

The radio continued behind him, the voice no longer indistinct. It named towns now. Roads. Instructions that came one after another in a steady sequence. The tone had not changed, but the content had narrowed, as if the voice were trying to move ahead of something already in motion.

He did not turn toward it.

He stepped away from the door and moved down the hallway, checking the adjacent rooms without fully entering them, as if the structure of the house might reveal something different from another angle. Everything else remained where it had been. Doors stood open or closed as expected. Nothing else had shifted. The change had not spread. It had concentrated itself here.

He returned to the door.

The wind struck the house again, harder this time, the impact carrying through the siding and into the frame with a low, sustained pressure. Something outside hit the wall—a dull, singular impact—and then the sound disappeared into the larger movement of air.

He placed his hand against the door once more, not pushing now, just confirming that it remained as it had been. The wood felt solid beneath his palm. Whatever held it from the other side had not shifted.

He stepped back and looked toward the front of the house.

The path was clear.

The idea formed quickly, not as a decision but as the next available movement. The room on the other side of the door had a window facing the side yard. The distance from the front door to that window was short. The house still allowed access from outside.

He turned and moved.

The front door opened without resistance. The air outside met him immediately, the wind no longer a background presence but a force that pressed against him from shifting directions. It did not move steadily. It struck, eased, and struck again, each interval different from the last.

He stepped out and turned along the side of the house, keeping close to the wall. His hand came up briefly to steady himself against it as the wind shifted his balance. The ground held firm beneath him, but the air did not allow a straight path. Each step required adjustment.

The window came into view.

He slowed as he approached it, not from hesitation but to see clearly through the glass. From the outside, the room appeared intact. The frame held. The glass was unbroken.

But the interior had changed.

The dresser was no longer against the wall. It stood angled toward the door. The bed had shifted, its alignment no longer parallel. Objects lay scattered across the floor, their positions irregular, as if they had been moved all at once rather than gradually displaced.

The door itself was out of view.

He raised his hand and struck the glass once. The sound carried inward, muted slightly by the thickness of it.

He called her name.

The wind took part of his voice and carried it away, stretching the sound so that it did not enter the room cleanly.

No answer came.

He struck the glass again, harder.

Still nothing.

He leaned closer, scanning the room, not looking for movement now but for any indication of where she might be. Nothing shifted. The objects remained where they had settled. The space held its disorder without revealing it.

He stepped back.

The decision came without hesitation.

He looked around the side of the house and picked up a loose object near the wall, heavy enough to carry force, small enough to control. He turned back toward the window, adjusted his grip, and lifted it.

The wind rose again, pressing against him as he brought the object forward.

He swung.

The glass shattered.

—

The glass broke inward under the force of the strike, the surface fracturing in a tight pattern before giving way, the center collapsing first and the rest following in jagged pieces that fell across the floor. The sound was sharp and brief, contained within the moment of impact, then replaced by the continuous movement of air as the opening allowed the wind to enter without obstruction.

He lowered the object and reached through, clearing the remaining shards from the bottom edge with the side of his forearm, pushing them aside just enough to make space. The glass cut into his skin in shallow lines, but he did not pause. He placed his hands against the frame and pulled himself through, shifting his weight carefully as he stepped into the room.

Inside, the air moved differently. It did not pass through in a single direction. It crossed the space in uneven currents, lifting lighter objects and shifting them slightly, then dropping them again as the force changed. The curtains snapped inward and fell back. Papers slid across the floor and caught against the legs of furniture.

The room itself held the shape he had seen from outside, but from within it, the displacement was more exact. The dresser had been driven at an angle toward the door, its weight pressed into it not evenly but along one edge, the top corner braced against the handle. The bed stood slightly turned, one side closer to the wall than the other. Smaller items had been moved without pattern—books, clothing, objects that no longer belonged where they had been placed.

The door remained closed.

He called her name again.

No answer came.

He moved toward the dresser and placed both hands against it. The surface was smooth beneath his palms, but the position of it told him what the resistance would be before he applied it. It had settled into place with weight behind it, its angle converting its own mass into pressure against the door.

He pushed.

The dresser did not move.

He adjusted his stance, widening his footing, lowering his center slightly so that the force came from his legs rather than his arms. He pushed again, steady this time, not striking at it but applying pressure that did not break.

The dresser shifted.

Not far. Not enough.

But enough to feel.

He held the pressure and continued, allowing the movement to carry forward instead of stopping and starting again. The legs scraped against the floor, catching briefly on debris, then sliding as the angle changed.

The door moved a fraction.

He pushed again.

The dresser gave a little more, its position no longer locked in the same way, the pressure against the handle loosening as the angle shifted.

The door opened slightly.

He stopped and looked through the gap.

The hallway beyond was no longer open.

The ceiling had dropped at an angle, a section of it pressing down into the space below, reducing the height of the passage. Debris lay across the floor—broken drywall, insulation, pieces of wood that had fallen and settled unevenly. The space did not close completely, but it narrowed into something that no longer allowed a straight path.

He called her name again.

This time, something answered.

A sound.

Not words.

Movement.

He held still, listening, separating it from the movement of air behind him, from the shifting of loose material, from the low strain in the structure above.

The sound came again.

Closer.

"Here."

Her voice carried through the space, thinner than it should have been, broken slightly as it passed through debris and moving air, but clear enough to recognize.

"I cannot open it," she said.

"I am here," he answered.

He returned to the dresser and pushed again, continuing the motion he had already begun, driving it further from the door. The resistance changed as the angle shifted, the weight no longer held in the same way.

The door opened wider.

The gap increased enough to see more of the hallway.

She stood there, partially visible beneath the lowered section of ceiling, her body angled within the narrowed space, one hand against the wall to steady herself. Dust marked her clothing where the structure had come down, and the floor beneath her feet was uneven with debris.

He saw her.

The fact of that did not change what stood between them.

He pushed once more, widening the opening as much as the dresser would allow, then moved toward the door and reached through the gap.

His hand extended into the space between them.

Her hand lifted.

Their fingers met.

He stepped into the hallway, placing his foot carefully between pieces of debris, lowering himself slightly to fit beneath the angled ceiling. The air felt different there—thicker, more contained, carrying the scent of broken material and dust.

He reached for her again and took her hand fully.

"I can pull you through," he said.

He shifted his footing, bracing himself, and pulled.

She moved slightly forward.

Then stopped.

The debris beneath her feet shifted, reducing her balance, preventing her from stepping cleanly into the opening. He adjusted his grip, tightening his hold, and pulled again, lowering his stance to anchor himself against the unstable surface.

She moved a little further.

Her shoulder reached the edge of the opening.

The space narrowed around her as she entered it.

For a moment, it held.

Then the structure above shifted.

Not suddenly. Not violently.

But enough.

The beam lowered slightly, changing the shape of the opening, reducing the space that had just allowed her forward.

Her movement stopped.

They remained connected, his hand around hers, her body partly within the opening, but the space no longer allowed continuation.

He held his position.

She held hers.

The opening remained.

But it did not widen further.

And what had been possible a moment before no longer was.

—

He tightened his grip on her hand, not pulling yet, but confirming that the connection held. Her fingers closed around his in response, the pressure steady, not strained, as if both of them understood that force alone would not determine what happened next. The space between them had narrowed into something specific, something that allowed contact but did not yet allow passage.

"I can get you through," he said, his voice low, directed toward her rather than into the space.

She shifted her weight slightly, testing the ground beneath her feet. The debris moved under her, small pieces sliding against one another, changing her footing without warning. She adjusted again, turning her body at an angle, bringing one shoulder forward in an attempt to align herself with the opening.

"I can try," she said.

He adjusted his stance, placing his feet more firmly against the floor behind him, one foot braced against a section of wall that remained intact, the other positioned to hold his balance if the debris beneath him shifted. The ceiling above pressed downward at an angle that forced him to lower himself, his shoulders angled slightly to remain within the available space.

He pulled.

She moved forward, her arm extending further into his reach, her shoulder entering the opening more fully this time. The debris beneath her shifted again, but held long enough for the movement to continue. Her body began to follow, turning as she moved, aligning with the narrow passage.

For a moment, the motion carried.

Then it slowed.

The space tightened around her, the beam above limiting the height, the debris beneath limiting the stability. Her movement reduced to small increments, each one dependent on how the surface beneath her responded.

He pulled again, steady, not sharply, maintaining a constant pressure rather than increasing it.

She moved a little further.

Her shoulder passed the narrowest part of the opening.

Her upper body followed.

The passage seemed possible.

Then the structure shifted.

The change was not abrupt, but it was unmistakable. The beam lowered slightly, altering the angle of the space, reducing the height just enough that the opening no longer matched the shape she had been moving through. The debris beneath her feet shifted at the same time, the pieces sliding, changing her balance.

Her movement stopped.

Not by hesitation.

By limit.

He felt the change through his grip, the tension in her arm no longer translating into forward motion. He held his position, maintaining the connection, waiting to see if the space would settle in a way that allowed continuation.

It did not.

"I cannot," she said.

The words came without panic, without strain, carrying only the fact of the space as it now existed.

He adjusted his footing again, lowering himself further, trying to create a different angle from which to pull. He shifted his grip slightly, tightening it, then pulled once more, testing whether the change in position might allow her to move.

She moved a fraction.

Then stopped.

The debris beneath her slid again, more this time, altering her stance enough that she had to hold her position to remain upright. The structure above responded with a low sound, not loud, but present, a strain carried through the material that did not resolve into collapse but did not remain neutral either.

He heard it.

He held still.

The sound settled into place.

Not worsening.

Not releasing.

Just there.

He looked upward briefly, enough to register the angle of the beam, the way it had come to rest against what remained of the wall, the weight it carried distributed across points that no longer aligned as they had been designed to. It was holding.

But not indefinitely.

He returned his attention to her.

"We can do this," he said.

She nodded slightly, the motion small, constrained by the space, but clear.

He tightened his grip and pulled again.

She moved forward, her upper body entering further into the opening, the alignment between her position and the space briefly restored. The debris beneath her held long enough to support the movement, and for a moment, the passage seemed to open again.

Then the structure shifted once more.

The beam lowered another fraction.

The opening reduced.

Her movement stopped again.

This time sooner.

The space no longer matched her position. It no longer allowed her forward without increasing the pressure against her from above and from the sides.

They remained connected, but the connection no longer carried movement.

He did not release her hand.

She did not withdraw hers.

They held the position that remained available to them, the space between them defined not by distance but by the shape of what could still occur.

The opening had not closed.

But it had become fixed.

And within that fixed space, the limit was clear.

—

They remained where they were, their hands joined across the narrowed opening, the connection steady even as the space around it continued to change. His grip held firm, not pulling now, not testing, simply maintaining contact as the structure above them settled further into place. The beam pressed lower by degrees that were small enough to watch but large enough to matter, reducing the height of the passage without collapsing it, fixing it into a position that no longer allowed movement through it.

She shifted her footing once, carefully, testing whether there was still a way to align her body with the space. The debris beneath her moved in response, fragments sliding against one another, altering her balance just enough that she had to stop again to steady herself. The movement did not bring her closer. It confirmed the limit.

He felt that through her hand, through the change in tension, through the absence of forward motion. He did not pull again. He did not try to force what the space no longer allowed. He held where he was, his body angled beneath the lowered ceiling, his weight balanced against a floor that no longer felt fully reliable.

"We need to move," he said, though the words carried less instruction than they once might have. They existed alongside the reality in front of them, not ahead of it.

She did not answer immediately. Her hand remained in his, her grip steady, not tightening, not loosening. Then she shifted slightly, not forward this time, but back, adjusting her position to something that could be maintained rather than advanced.

The structure above them responded again, the beam lowering another small amount, the change almost imperceptible until it was measured against where it had been moments before. Dust fell in a thin line from the edge where the ceiling had broken, drifting down between them and settling across their arms.

He looked upward briefly, then back to her.

"I can hold it," he said, though he did not reach for the beam this time. He knew the weight it carried. He had felt it before. There was no position from which he could change it enough to matter.

She shook her head, a small motion within the confined space.

"No," she said.

The word did not argue.

It named what was already there.

Their hands adjusted within the grip they shared, not withdrawing, but finding the position that could still hold. The contact had changed from something that might lead to movement into something that simply remained.

The debris beneath her shifted again, more noticeably this time, a small collapse of pieces settling under her weight. The change moved through her body and into his hand, altering the distance between them, reducing the reach that had been just enough.

He tightened his grip instinctively.

She held on.

For a moment, the connection held as it had.

Then it began to change.

Her arm moved back slightly, not by choice, but because the ground beneath her no longer supported the position she had been in. The opening between them narrowed again as the beam settled lower, the space tightening around the place where their hands met.

Their grip adjusted, sliding from full hand to fingers, the contact narrowing as the available space reduced.

He held on.

She held on.

The connection remained, but it no longer held the same shape.

Their fingers pressed together, the contact shifting to the smallest surface that could still maintain it. The movement between them slowed, not stopping all at once, but reducing until it could not continue.

Her fingers slipped.

Caught for a moment against his.

Then slipped again.

And then they were no longer connected.

Her hand moved back beyond the space he could reach, not disappearing from view, but no longer within the distance his body could cross. The opening remained, but it no longer joined them.

He stayed where he was, his hand still extended into the space where hers had been, the shape of the contact remaining in his fingers even as the connection itself had ended. He did not move immediately. There was nowhere to move into that would change what had already been set.

He called her name.

The sound carried into the space beyond the debris and the lowered beam, thinner now, shaped by the structure that separated them.

A faint sound came back.

Not words.

But presence.

She was still there.

But the distance between them no longer allowed what had almost happened.

He lowered his hand slowly, the motion controlled, as if releasing it too quickly might change something that had already been decided. The structure above them remained where it had settled, the opening fixed, the debris unmoving except for the small shifts caused by the air that continued to pass through the house.

He remained in the hallway a moment longer, then stepped back into the room, moving carefully through the debris, the broken glass, the objects that no longer belonged where they had been placed.

Outside, the wind continued.

Inside, the house held.

In the days that followed, the damage was assessed, then addressed. The broken window was covered. The debris was cleared. The section of ceiling that had collapsed was removed and rebuilt. The hallway was restored to its original height. The walls were repaired. The door was reset within its frame, the hinges checked, the latch aligned.

It opened.

It closed.

It held.

He used it again, moving through it as required, the motion outwardly unchanged. But there were moments when his hand would reach for the handle and pause just before turning it, his grip tightening slightly as if expecting resistance that was no longer there.

On one afternoon, standing alone in the hallway after the repairs had been completed, he closed the door and placed his hand against it. The surface felt solid beneath his palm, the wood unmoving, the frame steady. The latch sat cleanly within its place. There was no pressure against it.

Still, his hand remained there longer than necessary.

From another room, a door closed with a quiet, ordinary sound, and his body reacted before he could think, his shoulders tightening, his grip pressing briefly against the surface in front of him. The response passed, but it did not disappear.

At times, he left the door open longer than required, standing within the frame without crossing, his body aligned with the threshold while remaining still, as if waiting for something that did not come.

When people asked what had happened, he said that the door would not open.

The words were enough.

They held the part that could be spoken.

The rest remained where it had been formed.

He continued.

That is what remained.

STORY 3

The Hand That Slipped

Before the water rose high enough to erase the edges of things, the hand had been only a hand, part of the ordinary exchange through which bodies moved around one another without thought. It opened to carry, closed to grip, rested when nothing was required of it, and reached when something did. It did not yet hold meaning beyond function. It belonged to the order of small necessary acts by which one person steadied another, lifted something from a shelf, turned a handle, moved a chair, touched a shoulder, accepted a cup, fastened a coat, pointed toward a door. It existed within the body's work without asking to be remembered.

The house stood low enough that heavy weather always entered conversation before it entered the rooms. Rain was not unusual there. Water gathering at the edges of the yard was not unusual either. The ground sloped just enough to direct runoff toward the back, and the ditches beyond the road filled and emptied according to patterns people who lived there had learned not to fear too quickly. The house had been built with that knowledge in mind, its floor lifted slightly above the surrounding grade, its steps measured to create a small elevation that was not much to look at but had always been enough.

The road in front of it ran straight for a distance and then dipped where the land fell away toward the creek. Trees followed the line of the road in loose intervals, some close enough to shade the ditch, others set farther back behind fences and patches of open ground. The yards in that stretch of houses were not large, but they held what people needed them to hold: a place for bins, a place for tools, a place for chairs left out longer than intended, a place where children had once played and where adults still paused before going inside.

Inside, the rooms had been arranged less by design than by use. Furniture stood where it had stood for years, not because there was no other place for it, but because it had settled into the logic of the house and been left there long enough to seem fixed. The kitchen opened into the main room without full separation, the doorway between them wide enough that sound crossed easily and movement required no adjustment. A hallway extended from that shared space toward the bedrooms, narrow but sufficient, the walls close enough that carrying a box through it required a turn of the shoulders but not thought.

She had moved through that hallway so many times that her body no longer registered the dimensions of it. Her hand brushed the wall at the corner where the light switch sat, not because she needed it every time, but because repetition had made the gesture part of the turn. The paint there had dulled slightly from contact over the years, the surface changed by use without appearing worn from a distance. The rest of the wall remained intact, smooth enough, holding the same pale color that had been there through seasons of ordinary weather.

Outside, the rain had begun before morning but not with enough force to interrupt the pattern of the day. It moved across the roof in a steady sound that remained background rather than command, a continuous contact above the rooms that did not yet distinguish itself from other weather the house had already endured. The gutters took the first runoff cleanly. Water moved downward where it was meant to move downward. Nothing in that motion required response.

The radio was on, though low, its voice steady and procedural, delivering updates in language that did not yet alter the room. Streets were named. Water levels were mentioned. Advisories were repeated. The tone remained calm enough that the words did not immediately separate themselves from the rest of the morning. They entered the space and stayed there without yet demanding that anyone stand still and listen to them fully.

She moved from kitchen to hallway carrying a towel, then returned with an armful of things that had been left too low, placing them on the table without announcing why. The act did not yet rise to the level of urgency. It belonged instead to the category of early caution, the kind of motion people make while still hoping the precaution will prove unnecessary. A small bag was set near the chair by the door. Shoes were moved from the floor to the step by the wall. A charger was unplugged and wrapped around itself with more care than speed.

The water outside had begun to collect where the yard sloped away from the house, not in a rush but in a widening surface that reflected the changed light without yet appearing deep. The ditch by the road held more than it had the day before. The current in it moved fast enough to be seen now, carrying leaves and small debris with a direction that did not pause. What had earlier been rain had begun to gather into something else.

He stood at the front window and watched the edge of the road disappear first by degrees and then all at once, the line between pavement and ditch erased under moving water that no longer respected the shallower contours of the land. The change was visible enough now that it could not remain background. Still, the house held. The steps remained clear. The floor remained dry. The furniture sat where it had always sat. The body, encountering no disruption inside, was tempted to trust the continuity of the room over the evidence beyond it.

Another update came over the radio, this one more specific, naming the creek, naming the crossing, naming the expected rise with a precision that altered the air of the room without changing its contents. She turned toward it then and listened fully for the first time, her body holding still while the voice completed the advisory. He did not speak immediately after it ended. The silence that followed was not uncertainty exactly. It was recognition delayed by the fact that recognition required movement.

They began to lift what could be lifted. Not everything. Not yet. Only what the mind reached first when forced to sort in haste: papers, medication, photographs in frames that had already been dusted too many times, a small box from the closet shelf, the charger, the bag, the shoes, the radio itself. The sequence of selection did not follow value cleanly. It followed reach, memory, and habit. Objects nearest the hand became important because they were near. Things left behind were not judged unimportant so much as overtaken by the pace at which choosing had to occur.

The rain intensified. The sound on the roof deepened, not louder exactly, but heavier, the contact of water against the house changing in texture as the volume increased. Somewhere outside, something loose struck against something fixed and then struck again, the repeated sound making clear that the wind had shifted too. The front steps disappeared under a sheet of brown water that moved not with the contained direction of runoff but with the broader force of overflow. The threshold still held. The door remained dry. But the line at which outside became inside had begun to feel thinner than the wood and frame could account for.

She moved again toward the hallway, this time faster, bending to lift something from the floor near the bedroom door, then reaching higher toward a shelf where papers had been put away long enough ago to feel safe. Her hands moved quickly now, but not wildly. The room still imposed enough order that actions could be completed one at a time. The body continued to believe, even now, that sequence would hold.

Then the first intrusion came, not through the door but from beneath, a seep at the edge of the back room where the floor met the wall, a darkening line that spread before it could be named. It did not pour. It entered. The amount of it was small, the meaning of it larger. The house had not yet been overtaken, but it was no longer fully separate.

He crossed the room toward her then, calling her name in a voice that remained level even as the speed of his movement changed. The hallway had narrowed, not physically, but in urgency. Objects that earlier had been part of the ordinary arrangement now had to be avoided. The bag by the chair was lifted. The radio was turned higher. Another advisory came, less advisory now than warning.

The water at the back edge of the house spread quickly once it entered, not rising visibly at first so much as extending, covering more surface than seemed proportionate to its depth. The floor reflected it in uneven patches. A shoe left too low darkened. The hem of the towel she had dropped earlier touched it and wicked the damp upward. The change was no longer speculative. It had become material.

He reached the hallway just as she turned back toward him, her hands still full, one arm holding papers and the other reaching outward not because she had fallen, not yet, but because the floor beneath her had become less certain than it had been a moment before. The distance between them was short enough that neither believed it to be dangerous. The room still looked like a room. The walls held. The ceiling held. The doors remained in place. But the body knows before the mind consents when a surface has altered.

He put out his hand.

She reached with hers.

And for a moment, before the water rose higher, before the hallway became something else, before the body's confidence in the floor was broken and remade by force, the distance between them remained small enough to trust.

The contact formed cleanly at first, his hand closing around hers with the familiarity of something practiced so often that it required no adjustment. The grip did not yet carry urgency. It held weight, not force, their palms meeting, fingers aligning, the pressure between them enough to steady but not yet to pull. The distance across which the contact formed remained short, the space between their bodies still navigable within the ordinary logic of movement.

The floor beneath her shifted slightly, not visibly, but enough. The water that had entered at the back edge of the house did not rise all at once. It spread, moving across the surface in a thin layer that reduced friction before it increased depth. The boards beneath it remained where they had been, but the condition of them changed, the contact between foot and floor no longer holding in the same way. The first instability did not come from force. It came from loss of grip.

Her weight moved forward, not by intention, but by adjustment. The step she had begun did not complete as expected, the placement of her foot meeting a surface that did not respond with the same resistance. The motion shortened, then slid, the correction beginning before the imbalance fully formed. Her arm tightened against his hand, the pressure increasing as the body registered the change.

He responded immediately, though not abruptly, his grip closing more firmly, his stance widening slightly to absorb the shift. His feet remained on the drier section of the floor, the friction there still intact, his body able to hold its position without compensating for the same loss of stability. The connection between them transferred weight across that difference, her imbalance meeting his steadiness through the contact of their hands. He told her to hold on, the words carrying instruction rather than alarm, and she tightened her grip in response, her fingers closing further around his as the pressure became deliberate.

Behind her, the water spread further, the thin layer thickening incrementally as more entered through the seam at the back of the house. The surface of the floor reflected it unevenly, the light catching in irregular patches that moved as the water moved, making the ground appear less solid than it had been moments earlier. Objects near the edge of the room shifted slightly as the water reached them, small displacements that did not yet interrupt their position but marked the change.

Her foot slid again, this time further, and the correction required more effort. Her body leaned into the pull of his hand, the angle between them increasing as her center of gravity shifted away from where she had intended to place it. The movement was not a fall. It was the beginning of one, the point at which recovery still remained possible but no longer automatic. He pulled, not sharply, but with enough force to counter the direction of her movement, and the connection between them held as her body moved toward him, the distance closing slightly as the correction took effect.

Her other hand lifted instinctively, reaching for balance in the space beside her, finding nothing to hold. The wall remained just beyond reach, the objects along it too low or too unstable to provide support. The water continued to move, no longer spreading evenly but beginning to gather, the slight slope of the floor now working in reverse, drawing water inward and creating a shallow current that moved across the room with direction rather than diffusion. The force remained low, but it added to the instability, shifting the position of her feet as she tried to regain control.

He adjusted his stance again, stepping slightly backward to create a stronger base, his feet planted more firmly on the surface that remained less affected. The pull between them increased, the tension in their arms no longer neutral, the connection carrying weight rather than simply linking two positions. He told her to come toward him, the words measured rather than rushed, and she tried, lifting her foot and placing it again with caution, her body aware now that the surface beneath it could not be trusted in the same way.

The step shortened. The placement remained tentative. The weight transferred more slowly. The water shifted beneath her foot, reducing friction again and altering the contact before it could stabilize. Her foot slid sideways instead of forward, the correction misaligned, and her body tilted as the grip between them tightened further, the pressure in their hands increasing as the distance between stable and unstable widened.

He pulled again, this time more directly, drawing her toward the drier section of the floor, his movement controlled but more forceful than before. The distance between them closed slightly more, the space narrowing as she moved closer to his position. The water rose, not visibly at first, but enough that the depth increased just enough to change the movement beneath her feet, the surface no longer only reducing friction but beginning to carry her weight slightly, altering how her foot met the floor.

Her foot did not find purchase. It moved. Her balance followed. The correction did not complete. The grip between them held, but it stretched, the distance between their bodies increasing again, not because he had stepped back, but because her movement had carried her slightly away from him before the pull could correct it fully. The tension in their arms increased further, the connection now bearing more weight than it had been meant to.

He told her again, and she tried again. Her foot lifted, placed, and slid, the movement failing to resolve as the water beneath her shifted with a more defined current, moving across the floor with enough force to alter the direction of her step as it formed. The correction required more than balance. It required force she could not fully generate from where she stood.

He pulled harder. The connection held. Her body moved toward him again, but not cleanly, not in a straight line. The path between them had changed, the surface no longer allowing for direct movement, each step altered by the conditions beneath it. The distance closed, then opened again, the grip between them tightening further. Their hands remained joined, but the stability that had existed between them at the moment of contact had not returned, and the space across which that contact had to hold had begun to widen.

The motion did not remain contained to the moment of contact. It extended through the connection between them, the instability beneath her feet transferring upward into her body and across into his, the balance he had established beginning to adjust under the added weight. What had first required only steadiness now required effort, the difference between holding and pulling narrowing with each shift of her footing.

The water continued to rise, not in a sudden surge but in a steady increase that altered the condition of the floor more than its appearance. The surface remained visible, the boards still discernible beneath the thin layer, but the behavior of that surface had changed. Each step she attempted met a condition that did not hold long enough to support it, the contact between her foot and the floor shifting before it could stabilize, the timing of her movement no longer aligned with the resistance she expected.

He adjusted again, stepping back another half pace to maintain his position on the drier section, his body compensating for the pull now placed on his arm. The movement was controlled, but it altered the distance between them, increasing the span across which the connection had to hold. The grip tightened further, their fingers interlocking more firmly, the pressure no longer incidental but necessary. He told her to stay with him, his voice still even, though the strain had entered it.

She tried to respond, but the effort of maintaining her footing occupied her fully. Her body shifted forward again, not in a step but in a slide that she attempted to correct mid-motion, her weight transferring unevenly as the floor beneath her failed to meet it with consistency. The movement did not resolve into a fall, but it did not return to stability either.

The water moved with more direction now, no longer spreading evenly but flowing across the floor with a shallow current that intersected her stance at an angle. The force of it remained low, but it was continuous, enough to alter the position of her feet as she tried to place them, enough to disrupt the correction before it could complete. The interaction between her movement and the current created a misalignment that compounded with each attempt to regain balance.

He pulled again, more firmly this time, the effort visible in the tension along his arm, his shoulder drawing back to counter the direction of her movement. The connection held, but the pull did not translate cleanly into her motion. Her body moved toward him, then shifted sideways as the water redirected her footing, the path between them no longer straight. The distance closed slightly, then opened again, and the rhythm between them broke.

Her free hand reached outward again, this time finding the edge of the wall for a moment, her fingers brushing against the surface without securing it. The contact was brief, insufficient to support her weight, and it disappeared as her body shifted again under the influence of the water. The wall remained where it had been. It did not move closer. It did not offer more than its surface.

The water deepened incrementally, the level rising just enough to begin carrying small objects, the edge of a mat lifting and shifting, the corner of a paper moving from where it had been placed. The change remained subtle, but it altered the environment in ways that made each movement less predictable.

He stepped again, adjusting his position to maintain traction, his feet seeking the last areas of the floor that still held without slipping. The movement created more distance between them, not because he intended it, but because maintaining his own stability required it. The span between his hand and hers lengthened, the angle of their arms increasing, the connection stretched further across the space. He told her again to come toward him, the words steady but more urgent now, and she tried.

Her foot lifted, placed, and slid, the motion repeating without resolving, each attempt to step forward redirected by the surface beneath her. The current carried her slightly off line each time, her body compensating in ways that did not align with his pull. The effort increased, but the result did not. He pulled harder, and the connection held as her body moved toward him again, the distance narrowing briefly, the alignment improving just enough to suggest that the movement might complete.

For a moment, the tension between them translated into motion that followed a direct path, her body drawn closer, her footing almost finding enough stability to carry her forward, but the floor shifted beneath her again, not visibly, but enough. Her foot slid sideways instead of forward, the correction misaligned, her weight transferring into a direction that did not bring her closer to him. The movement broke the partial alignment they had achieved, the path between them disrupted again.

The grip between them tightened further, their fingers pressing together with enough force to maintain contact even as the tension increased, the connection now bearing more weight than it had been meant to carry. The muscles in his arm tightened, his shoulder drawing back further, his stance widening again to absorb the strain. The water rose again, the change incremental but cumulative, the depth now sufficient to alter not only friction but buoyancy in small ways, lifting the edge of her step, reducing the contact between foot and floor just enough to make each placement less secure than the last.

She tried again, her foot lifting, placing, and sliding as the motion failed to complete, the connection holding but straining, the distance between them increasing again not through a single movement, but through a series of small misalignments that accumulated. Each one widened the gap by a fraction that did not reverse. He pulled again, harder now, the effort visible, the control still present but under pressure, his body working to maintain the connection against forces that did not respond to him directly.

Her body moved, then shifted, then resisted—not by intention, but by condition—and the path between them no longer existed as a straight line. It had become a series of corrections that did not resolve into forward movement. Their hands remained joined, but the stability that had once existed between them had been replaced by a tension that could not be fully controlled, the connection holding across a space that no longer behaved in ways either of them could fully predict, and still it held, for the moment, across the widening distance.

He did not move for a moment after the pattern shifted beyond what he could track as a sequence. The connection between them remained, but it no longer functioned as it had when it first formed. What had begun as a steady hold had become a line under strain, the tension carried through their arms no longer balanced, the weight between them uneven and shifting.

The water continued to rise, the change incremental but constant, altering the conditions of the floor in ways that did not reverse. The surface beneath her feet no longer offered any reliable resistance. Each attempt to place her weight resulted in movement before stability could form, the contact between her body and the ground disrupted before it could hold. The current moved across the floor with more definition now, not strong enough to push her directly, but sufficient to interfere with every correction she attempted.

He adjusted again, stepping back slightly to maintain traction, his position shifting to compensate for the increasing pull. The movement widened the distance between them, not by intention but by necessity, his body seeking stability even as he tried to reduce the span across which their connection had to hold. The angle of their arms increased, the line between them tightening as it stretched, and he told her again to stay with him, his voice controlled, though the effort required to keep it that way had increased.

She tried to move toward him, but the attempt did not translate into forward motion. Her foot lifted, placed, and slid again, the sequence repeating without resolving, each step redirected by the conditions beneath it. The water shifted around her, altering the position of her footing before it could settle, the interaction between movement and surface no longer predictable.

He pulled, harder now, the effort visible in the tension of his stance, his body leaning back to counter the force drawing her away. The connection held, but it did not produce the result he intended. Her body moved toward him for a fraction, then shifted sideways, the current altering her path before the motion could complete. The distance between them narrowed, then widened again, the pattern repeating without progress.

Her free hand reached outward again, searching for something that might hold, her fingers extending toward the wall, the edge of a piece of furniture, any surface that could provide resistance. For a moment, she found the corner of a shelf, her hand closing around it just long enough to register contact, but the object shifted under her weight, its position not fixed strongly enough to support her, and the hold failed before it could stabilize her movement.

The water deepened further, the change subtle in appearance but significant in effect. The surface no longer only reduced friction. It carried her weight in small, uneven ways, lifting her foot slightly as she tried to plant it, reducing the pressure that might have allowed her to regain balance. The floor had not disappeared, but its function had altered beyond recognition.

He stepped again, seeking a firmer position, his feet finding less and less ground that could be trusted. The movement increased the distance between them once more, the span stretching further, the tension in their arms intensifying as the connection bore more of her weight. He told her again to come toward him, the instruction steady but now carrying urgency that could no longer be contained entirely.

She tried again, her body committing more fully to the movement, her foot lifting higher before placing, her weight transferring more quickly in an attempt to overcome the instability. For a moment, the motion aligned, her body moving toward him in a more direct path, the distance closing enough to suggest that the connection might succeed, but the surface shifted again beneath her, not visibly, but enough, and her foot did not hold. It moved sideways, the alignment broke, and her weight transferred into a direction that did not bring her closer, the correction failing before it could take effect as the partial progress disappeared and the distance opened again through compounding misalignment.

The grip between them tightened further, their fingers pressing together with force now, the connection no longer a hold but a strain, the muscles in his arm pulled taut, his shoulder braced, his stance widening again to absorb the increasing load. The effort required to maintain the connection had grown beyond what either of them had anticipated when their hands first met, and the water continued to rise, not dramatically, but enough to change the balance again, the depth increasing just enough to reduce the stability of every movement she attempted, the current shifting slightly and altering the direction of force across the floor so that the angle of her stance no longer aligned with his pull.

He pulled again, harder, the effort now visible in the full engagement of his body, his weight shifting backward, his feet pressing into the last sections of the floor that still held. The connection held, but the response did not follow. Her body moved toward him, then away again, the path between them disrupted by the shifting surface, their hands remaining joined even as the distance between them increased beyond what the connection had been meant to carry, the line of their arms stretching further, the angle sharper, the tension constant and rising.

The balance that had once existed between them had been replaced by a condition in which neither could fully control the outcome, the forces acting on them no longer aligned with their movement. She tried again, her foot lifting, placing, and sliding as the motion repeated without producing change, while he held and she held, the connection remaining even as it no longer brought them closer, the space between them widening not through a single movement but through the accumulation of many small failures to align, each one adding distance that did not return as the water continued to move, the floor continued to shift, and the connection held while the limit approached.

He remained where he was as the strain between them reached a point that no longer allowed for further adjustment, the connection still holding but no longer able to translate effort into movement. The tension in his arm had become constant, no longer rising and falling with each attempt but sustained, the weight he carried through the grip fixed in place as the conditions beneath her feet continued to shift beyond what either of them could correct.

The water rose again, not in a visible surge but in a continued increase that altered the surface in ways that compounded every instability already present. The floor no longer behaved as a surface that could be worked against. It had become something that moved in response to pressure, the contact between foot and ground changing before it could be used, the current beneath her carrying each attempt at correction slightly off its intended path.

He pulled again, though the motion had changed, the effort no longer directed toward drawing her closer in a straight line but toward holding her in place against the widening instability. The connection held, their hands still joined, their fingers locked with a force that had moved beyond intention into necessity, but the result did not change, her body shifting toward him and then away again, the movement no longer resolving into progress but repeating within the same constrained pattern.

The distance between them increased by small degrees that did not reverse, each misalignment adding to the space across which their connection had to hold, the angle of their arms sharpening further, the line between them no longer level but pulled taut, the strain carried through muscle and bone rather than position, the effort to maintain the connection now continuous rather than something that could be applied in intervals.

She tried again to step, her body committing to the motion with what remained of her balance, her foot lifting and placing with greater force as if force alone might compensate for the instability beneath it. For a moment, the movement aligned enough to suggest that the distance might close, her body shifting toward him in a path that held longer than before, but the surface changed again, the water redirecting her footing before the motion could complete, and the alignment failed once more as her weight transferred sideways without correction and the connection stretched further.

He felt the change immediately, the increase in tension moving through his arm as her balance shifted beyond what his position could fully counter, and he adjusted his stance again, though there was little left to adjust, his feet already placed at the edge of what the floor could offer, his body working to maintain a hold that no longer had a stable point to draw toward. He told her to hold, though the word had changed and no longer functioned as instruction but as effort itself, and she held, but the holding no longer preserved the distance between them and only delayed its widening.

The water continued to move, the current now more defined, carrying force across the floor in a direction that did not align with his pull, the angle between their bodies increasing as the conditions beneath her shifted further away from what he could influence. The floor no longer provided resistance that could be used. It provided only instability that had to be endured, and their hands remained joined even as the connection had begun to change, the grip tightening beyond comfort, the pressure between their fingers increasing as the strain grew, the contact no longer neutral but a point at which force accumulated without release, the skin compressed, the joints adjusting under load, the connection bearing more than it had been meant to carry.

He pulled again, the effort complete and the result unchanged, her body moving toward him for a fraction before shifting away again as the motion was redirected by the water before it could complete, the path between them breaking again into angles that did not align, the distance widening further, not dramatically but enough that the strain increased beyond what could be sustained without consequence. The first slip did not come from release but from change within the grip itself, her fingers adjusting under the increasing pressure, the contact shifting slightly as the strain altered the position of their hands, the movement small but sufficient to change how their grip held.

He felt it, adjusted, tightened further, and for a moment the connection stabilized again, the grip reforming under greater pressure, the hold reasserted through force alone, but the conditions beneath her did not change, her foot moving again, the current shifting again, her balance following, the tension increasing once more. The second slip followed, her fingers losing a fraction of their hold as the strain exceeded the position they could maintain, the contact reducing but not breaking, the surface between their hands decreasing as the grip compressed beyond what could be sustained evenly.

He pulled again, harder, the effort complete, the connection responding but not fully, her body moving and then shifting away again, the distance widening further, the third slip not arriving as a separate event but as the continuation of the others, the cumulative result of strain, movement, and misalignment, their fingers still joined but no longer holding with the same surface of contact, the grip reduced from full hand to partial hold, the connection narrowing even as the force within it increased.

He did not release, and she did not let go, but the connection no longer occupied the same space, the water moving again, the floor shifting again, the alignment breaking again, and this time the correction did not follow, their fingers holding for a moment longer at the edge of contact, the pressure concentrated into a smaller point as the rest of the grip gave way, the connection reduced to the last place where force could still be carried before it slipped—not suddenly, not completely at once, but in a motion that completed itself once it began, their fingers losing contact not by choice but by the condition that had formed around them, the separation occurring as the force between them exceeded what the contact could sustain.

Her hand moved away, not by intention but by the absence of what had held it, and he remained where he was, his hand still extended into the space where hers had been, the shape of the grip held in his fingers even after the contact had gone, the tension in his arm not releasing immediately but remaining for a moment longer as the body held the position it had been in before the connection ended, and then it released, the space between them remaining, no longer crossed, while the water continued to move, the floor continued to shift, and the hand that had held had slipped.

STORY 4

The Last Words Spoken

BEFORE THE STORM TURNED language into something that had to compete with noise, the last words had not yet separated themselves from all the others that filled an ordinary day. Speech moved through the house the way movement did, passing from one room to another without requiring formal notice, carrying instruction, question, reply, correction, habit, and the small acknowledgments by which people confirmed each other's presence. A voice called from the kitchen to the back room. Another answered from the hallway. A name spoken once could serve as summons, warning, affection, or impatience depending on tone, and tone changed quickly enough within a day that meaning did not always need to be fixed in the words themselves. Most of what was said disappeared as soon as it was heard, not because it lacked importance, but because it belonged to the flow of use rather than memory.

The house stood close enough to the road that passing vehicles could be heard distinctly but not so close that they interrupted the rooms within it. The yard between the porch and the ditch had been crossed often enough that the grass no longer held evenly, two worn paths marking where feet had preferred to go, one toward the drive, the other toward the side gate that led to the back. The porch railing had been painted more than once, the newest coat laid over earlier layers that weather had roughened but not erased, and the front steps dipped slightly at the center from years of weight meeting them in the same place. Nothing about the house suggested grandeur. It held instead the settled clarity of a place used long enough to become specific, a place where objects remained because they belonged to the order that had formed around them.

Inside, the rooms were arranged according to necessity and repetition rather than design. The kitchen opened into the main room without full separation, the threshold between them wide enough that sound traveled easily and movement required no pause. The hallway extending toward the bedrooms narrowed the further it went, not visibly enough to matter when walking through it empty, but enough that carrying a basket or a box required the body to turn slightly at the shoulders. The walls there bore the marks of use softened by time, the edges where furniture had brushed them touched up unevenly, the corner by the light switch dulled from hands finding it without looking.

The day had begun under a sky that looked unsettled without yet appearing dangerous. The light held, but not cleanly. It spread across surfaces without sharpening edges, flattening distance in a way that made the street beyond the window seem nearer and less distinct at the same time. The radio had been on since morning, its volume low enough that the words moved through the rooms as background rather than command. Streets were named. Water levels were mentioned. Advisories were repeated. The tone remained procedural, and because it remained procedural, it allowed the mind to delay full recognition. Information entered the space without yet altering the sequence of actions taking place within it.

She moved between the kitchen and the back room carrying small things first, not because they mattered most, but because they were nearest. A towel left too low was lifted and hung over a chair. A bag was placed by the front door. A charger was unplugged and wrapped around itself with more care than speed. The motions belonged less to emergency than to anticipation, the kind of early caution by which people try to prepare without fully admitting what they are preparing for. He watched some of this from the window and some of it only by hearing the sounds of it: a drawer opened and shut, a cabinet door closing, an object placed on a table with enough weight to be heard but not enough to signify alarm.

Outside, the rain moved steadily across the roof, its sound consistent enough that it almost disappeared into the structure of the morning. Water in the ditch by the road had risen, but ditches rose and fell according to rhythms people who lived near them learned not to fear too quickly. The ground sloped toward the back of the lot, and runoff usually found its path there. The house had been built with that knowledge in mind, its floor slightly elevated above the yard, its steps enough to create distinction between weather outside and dry ground within. That distinction had held before. It still held now.

He stood with one hand against the window frame and watched the edge of the road lose its definition as runoff spread over the shallow depression beside it. The water moved with more direction than before, carrying leaves, small branches, and the pale debris that rain pulls from places where it has sat too long. What had earlier been scattered weather had begun to organize itself into force. Still, the house remained unchanged. The floor was dry. The furniture remained where it had always been. The sounds inside continued in their usual order. The body, finding continuity within the room, wanted to trust the room more than the evidence beyond it.

Another advisory came over the radio, this one more specific, naming the creek, naming the crossing, naming the expected rise in a way that altered the air of the room even before it altered anyone's movement. She stopped then and listened fully for the first time, her body held still while the voice completed the update. He did not speak immediately after it ended. The silence that followed was not disbelief. It was the pause required when what has been possible in theory begins to enter the range of what must be acted upon.

They began to gather what could be gathered quickly. Not everything. Only what the hand reached first when time had not yet run out but had ceased to feel abundant: medication, papers, framed photographs, a small box from a shelf, a set of keys moved from one surface to another so they would not be forgotten. The logic of the choosing did not entirely follow value. Nearness ruled some of it. Habit ruled more. Objects closest to the hand became important because they were there. What remained behind did not become unimportant. It simply waited too long to be chosen.

The rain intensified without changing into anything spectacular. It did not announce itself through violence but through persistence. The sound on the roof deepened in texture, heavier now, the contact of water against the house no longer incidental. Somewhere outside, something loose struck against something fixed and then struck again, the repeated sound marking a change in the wind. The front steps disappeared beneath a sheet of brown water moving not with the contained direction of runoff but with the broader force of overflow. The threshold still held.

The door remained dry. Yet the line by which inside remained inside had begun to feel thinner than the materials of the house could account for.

She crossed the room more quickly then, speaking as she moved, not to begin an argument or to explain, but to keep the sequence of action shared between them. He answered from the window, then from the middle of the room, then not at all as he bent to lift something from the floor and set it higher. Their words moved past one another and through one another, fragments of practical exchange that did not yet know they were moving toward a boundary. A question was asked about the bag by the chair. A reply came from the back room. A name was spoken once more, without urgency yet, only direction. Language still believed it had time.

The first intrusion came quietly, not through the front door but from the back edge of the house where the floor met the wall. A dark line appeared there and spread before either of them named it, the water entering not as a rush but as an insistence. It did not need volume to alter the room. The amount of it remained small. The meaning of it did not.

She turned toward it first, bending to lift what was still low enough to be reached without thinking. He crossed the room toward her then, his pace changing not into panic but into focus, the body narrowing itself around one direction. The hallway, the back room, the chair by the door, the table now holding too many necessary things—everything that had earlier belonged to the ordinary arrangement of the house had begun to change function. Objects had become obstacles or priorities according to where they stood.

The water spread quickly once it entered, not deep enough at first to resist movement but enough to alter the surface beneath it. The floor reflected it in uneven patches. A shoe left too low darkened. The edge of the towel she had placed on the chair earlier touched it and began to wick the damp upward. The room still looked like a room. The walls held. The ceiling held. The doors remained where they had always been. Yet the body, encountering the first instability in the floor beneath it, registered the change before thought gave it language.

He called to her then. She answered, though the sound of the rain and the radio and the water entering had begun to interfere with the easy travel of voices across the house. What was said still mattered. But each phrase now had to cross more than distance. It had to cross distraction, pressure, urgency, and the first interruption of noise.

She moved toward him, one arm full, the other reaching back for something she had not meant to leave. He moved toward her from the opposite direction, his hand already lifting before the distance between them required it. The floor between them remained only a few steps wide. The house still held them within the same room, within the same line of sight, within the same possibility of correction.

Their mouths opened again.

And whatever came next would not remain only words.

The words that followed did not arrive as a single exchange but as a continuation of what had already been in motion, fragments of instruction and response crossing the room with enough clarity to be understood but no longer with the ease that had defined them earlier. The distance between them remained short, but the conditions through which sound traveled had changed, the rain on the roof deepening, the water moving across the floor adding a second layer of noise, and the radio continuing its steady delivery without adjusting to the urgency within the room.

He said her name again, more directly now, the sound placed with intention rather than habit, and she answered, though not immediately, her attention divided between what she held and what she still believed she could retrieve. The exchange did not pause long enough to become silence. It continued, but the continuity had begun to fracture, each phrase requiring more effort to send and more effort to receive.

She told him she had what she needed, though her movement suggested otherwise, her body turning slightly as if still oriented toward the back room even as she stepped toward him. He answered that it was enough, that what remained could remain, the words shaped by urgency but not yet by finality. The meaning of enough had changed, but neither of them paused to define it.

The water spread further across the floor, the thin layer deepening just enough to alter how sound moved within the room. Footsteps no longer met the boards with the same clarity. The contact between foot and surface softened, the sound of movement absorbed into the water rather than carried cleanly across the space. Their voices had to compete with that change, the subtle loss of sharpness making each word less distinct even when spoken at the same volume.

He stepped toward her again, his path no longer direct, the objects between them requiring adjustment, the chair by the door now positioned differently than it had been earlier, the bag at its base shifting slightly as the water reached it. He said something about the door, about moving forward, about leaving what could not be carried, but the phrasing did not complete itself in a single line. It came in parts, each phrase shaped by movement as much as by thought.

She answered him, but the words did not arrive intact. He caught enough of them to understand her intention, something about the papers, something about the back room, something about returning for what had not yet been lifted. The meaning was clear even where the language was not. The sequence of action she held in mind had not yet collapsed into the necessity he had already accepted.

The radio voice rose slightly, not louder but more insistent, the cadence tightening as locations were repeated, as instructions replaced advisories. The sound filled the room in a way that no longer allowed it to remain background. It intersected with their voices, not replacing them but complicating them, each word spoken within the house now moving through a layer of speech that did not belong to either of them.

He told her again to come, the word shorter this time, less shaped by explanation and more by direction. She said something in return, a phrase that began clearly but lost its edges before it reached him, the rain and the radio and the water on the floor breaking it apart as it crossed the distance. He understood enough to know she had not yet left behind what she still held in mind.

The water rose again, the increase small but sufficient to change the rhythm of their movement. The floor beneath her feet no longer responded with the same resistance, the contact shifting before it could stabilize, her step shortening as she adjusted. The change did not stop her movement, but it altered it, the timing of each step no longer matching what she expected.

He moved closer, closing the distance between them by a fraction, his hand lifting again as if the act of reaching might complete what the words could no longer secure. He said her name once more, and this time the sound carried through the room with enough clarity to reach her without breaking. She looked toward him then, fully, her attention leaving the back room and returning to the space between them.

She said something then that he heard clearly, though later he would not be certain of its exact wording, only of its structure, the way it placed something behind her and something ahead of her in relation to him. It was not a long sentence. It did not require one. It marked a shift from what could be retrieved to what must be left.

He answered, though the word he chose did not carry the full weight of what he meant. It was a brief acknowledgment, a confirmation rather than a correction, the kind of word used when agreement must be established quickly. It held them in the same direction, even if it did not fully express the change that had already occurred.

The room continued to fill with sound, the rain constant, the radio insistent, the water moving with a soft, continuous motion across the floor. Their voices moved through it all, still present, still functional, but no longer primary. Each phrase had to be placed more deliberately to be heard, each response shaped by the need to cross interference.

She took another step toward him, the movement careful now, her foot placed with more attention, the surface beneath it no longer reliable. He moved toward her at the same time, their paths aligning more directly for the first time since the water had entered. The distance between them shortened again, the space narrowing to something that could be crossed.

He said one more thing then, a phrase that combined instruction and reassurance without separating them, something about coming forward, about not turning back, about the door, about leaving what remained. The words did not carry fully intact across the room, but their direction did.

She answered him again, and this time he caught only the beginning of it, the first word clear, the rest dissolving into the noise that now filled the house. The meaning reached him anyway, carried less by the sound itself than by the alignment of her movement with his.

Their voices continued.

But each word now had to cross a room that was no longer neutral.

And each phrase arrived carrying less of itself than it had when it was spoken.

The exchange between them did not end when the words became harder to hear. It changed, the language no longer carrying itself cleanly across the space, the meaning forced to travel through movement, timing, and the narrowing alignment of their bodies rather than through sound alone. What was said remained present, but it no longer arrived whole. Each phrase reached the other incomplete, requiring the rest to be supplied by what could be seen.

He moved closer, reducing the distance between them by another step, his path adjusted around the objects that had shifted out of place. The chair near the door had moved slightly, its position altered by the water gathering beneath it, the bag at its base lifting just enough to tilt against one leg. He stepped around it without looking down, his attention fixed on her, his hand still extended, though it had not yet reached her.

She moved toward him at the same time, her steps shortened by the change in the floor, her weight transferred more carefully, her body no longer trusting the surface to hold without adjustment. The water had deepened enough now that each step produced resistance and drift at once, her foot meeting the floor and then sliding slightly before settling, the motion requiring correction before the next could begin.

He said her name again, and this time the word reached her intact, the sound carrying across the space with enough clarity to stand apart from the noise. She answered, though the reply did not fully return, the beginning audible, the rest broken by the radio's continued voice and the constant pressure of rain against the house. The meaning held, even where the language did not.

The radio had changed tone without raising volume, the cadence tighter now, the repetition more frequent, the instructions no longer spaced but layered, one following another with less pause between them. The voice named locations, named rising levels, named routes that might still hold. The words entered the room without waiting to be received, intersecting with everything else that was being said.

He spoke again, a shorter phrase this time, the structure reduced to what could be carried quickly: come now, leave it, this way. The words did not all arrive at once. Some reached her. Others dissolved. The direction remained clear.

She responded, but her voice had to pass through more than distance now. It moved through water, through sound, through urgency that altered how quickly she spoke and how quickly she moved. He caught enough to understand that she had stopped reaching backward, that her attention had turned fully toward him, that what remained behind her had been left.

The water continued to rise, not dramatically, but enough to change the sound of the room again. The floor no longer reflected noise. It absorbed and redirected it, the movement of water across the boards creating a continuous, low interference that filled the space between them. Their voices no longer crossed an open room. They crossed a field of sound that altered them as they passed through it.

He stepped forward again, closing the distance further, his hand now within reach of hers though not yet in contact. He said something then that he did not repeat, a phrase that combined urgency with something else, something that did not belong entirely to instruction. It was longer than what he had said before, and because it was longer, less of it arrived. The beginning reached her. The end did not.

She answered with a single word that carried more clearly than anything she had said since the water entered, not because it was louder, but because it was shorter, the sound able to move through the interference without breaking. He heard it. He understood it. The meaning did not require expansion.

They moved toward each other again, the distance between them now reduced to what could be crossed in a single step if the floor had remained as it had been. But it had not. The surface beneath them altered each placement, each step slowed by the need to correct before continuing, each movement shaped by the conditions that now defined the room.

He reached.

She reached.

Their hands came close enough that the space between them narrowed to inches, the contact almost formed, the connection nearly complete. He said one more word then, something that might have been her name again or might have been something else shaped into the same sound, and she answered, though the reply did not carry fully, the sound breaking before it reached him.

The radio voice rose again within the same volume, the repetition of instruction now continuous, the layering of phrases making it difficult to distinguish one from another. The rain pressed harder against the roof, the sound deepening, the water on the floor moving with more direction, the current now visible in the way it carried small objects from one side of the room to the other.

Their hands hovered in the space between them, close enough to see the lines in each other's skin, close enough to feel the movement of air displaced by the water and their own motion. He spoke again, but the word did not arrive. She spoke again, and the same happened. The exchange had reached a point at which language no longer crossed the distance in full.

What remained of their communication shifted.

It moved into timing.

Into direction.

Into the shared understanding of what had to happen next.

He stepped forward again.

She did the same.

The distance closed.

Their hands met.

The contact formed.

And whatever words followed did not remain whole long enough to be remembered as they had been spoken.

The contact between their hands formed in the space where language had already begun to fail, the grip closing not as a continuation of what had been said, but as a replacement for it. What words had been carrying, the hand now held. The pressure between them increased immediately, not gradually, the connection taking on weight as soon as it formed, their fingers tightening around one another as the conditions beneath them continued to shift.

The water moved more forcefully across the floor now, no longer spreading but carrying, the shallow current intersecting their stance at an angle that altered every adjustment they attempted to make. The surface beneath their feet did not hold long enough to support a full step, the contact breaking slightly before it could stabilize, each movement requiring correction before the next could begin. The room had not changed in its structure, but it had changed in how it could be moved through, the path between them no longer defined by distance alone but by the instability that filled it.

He pulled, not sharply, but with sustained force, the motion directed toward closing the remaining space between them, his body aligning behind the effort as he stepped back slightly to create leverage. The movement was controlled, but it altered the distance in a way that required her to follow, the connection between them carrying not just contact but direction. She responded, her body shifting toward him, her footing uncertain, the step she attempted shortened by the movement beneath it.

The water rose again, the increase small but sufficient to change the way her foot met the floor, the surface no longer offering resistance but responding to pressure by moving with it. The contact between her foot and the boards beneath became momentary, each placement sliding before it could settle, the timing of her movement no longer aligned with the stability she expected. The correction required more effort than the step itself.

He said something then, a word or phrase that might have been instruction, might have been reassurance, but it did not carry intact. The sound left his mouth, entered the space between them, and broke before it reached her, the rain and the radio and the movement of water absorbing it into the larger noise of the room. She answered, though what she said followed the same path, the meaning present in her movement more than in the sound itself.

The connection between their hands tightened further, their grip adjusting under the increasing strain, their fingers pressing together with more force as the distance between stable and unstable widened. The line of their arms sharpened, no longer level but angled, the tension carried through muscle rather than position. The hold that had formed between them now bore weight that neither of them could fully control.

He stepped again, drawing her toward him, his movement measured but more forceful than before, the effort visible in the way his body braced against the shifting floor. The distance between them closed by a fraction, the space narrowing enough to suggest that the connection might complete what the words had not. She moved with the pull, her body aligning more directly for a moment, her footing finding enough stability to carry her forward.

Then the surface changed again.

Her foot did not hold.

It shifted sideways, the correction misaligned, her weight transferring into a direction that did not bring her closer. The motion broke the partial alignment they had achieved, the distance opening again even as the connection between them remained.

He pulled harder, the effort now fully engaged, his stance widening, his weight shifting backward to counter the movement that drew her away. The connection held, but the path between them no longer followed a straight line. Her body moved toward him, then away again, the current beneath her redirecting her footing before the motion could complete. The distance between them narrowed and widened in succession, the pattern repeating without resolution.

The water deepened, the change still incremental but now sufficient to alter not only friction but buoyancy, the edge of her step lifted slightly as she tried to place it, reducing the pressure that might have allowed her to stabilize. The floor had not disappeared, but it no longer functioned as something that could be relied upon to resist her movement. It responded instead, shifting with her, carrying part of her weight away from the point where it could be used.

He said her name again, and though the word did not carry fully, the shape of it reached her, enough to draw her attention forward, enough to align her movement once more with his. She answered, but the reply did not arrive in full, the sound breaking as it crossed the space, leaving only the beginning intact.

They moved again.

Together this time, but not evenly.

He pulled.

She stepped.

The connection held.

The distance changed.

But did not close.

The strain between them increased, not through a single motion, but through the accumulation of many small failures to align, each one widening the space by a fraction that did not return. Their hands remained joined, but the stability that had once existed between them had been replaced by a tension that could not be resolved through effort alone.

The radio continued.

The rain continued.

The water continued to move across the floor.

Their voices did not stop.

But they no longer carried what they had at the beginning.

The connection between them held.

And the words began to disappear inside it.

The connection between their hands held as the space for language closed, the grip carrying what words could no longer complete. What had been spoken remained within the moment, but it no longer traveled forward in the same way, the exchange between them shifting fully into contact, into timing, into the shared recognition of what was happening even as the ability to name it diminished.

The water continued to rise, the increase steady enough that it did not shock the body into panic, but constant enough that each second altered the conditions of the last. The floor no longer functioned as a surface that could be worked against. It moved in response to pressure, shifting beneath each step, reducing the contact between foot and ground before it could be used, the current carrying force across the room with direction now, not strong enough to push them directly but sufficient to interfere with every correction they attempted to make.

He pulled again, though the motion had changed from drawing her closer to holding her within reach, the effort sustained rather than applied in bursts. The connection held, their hands still joined, their fingers locked with a force that had moved beyond intention into necessity, but the result did not change, her body moving toward him and then away again, the motion redirected by the water before it could resolve into progress. The distance between them increased in small increments that did not reverse, each misalignment adding to the span across which their connection had to hold, the angle of their arms sharpening further, the line between them pulled taut, the strain carried through muscle and bone rather than position, the effort to maintain the connection becoming continuous rather than something that could be applied and released.

He said something then, a word or phrase that did not arrive intact, the sound breaking as it crossed the space between them and dissolving into the rain, the radio, and the movement of water. She answered, though what she said followed the same path, the meaning carried not by the words themselves but by the way she held his hand and tried to move toward him. She stepped again, her body committing to the motion with what remained of her balance, her foot lifting and placing with more force as if force might compensate for the instability beneath it, and for a moment the movement aligned, her body moving toward him in a path that held long enough to suggest that the distance might close, before the surface shifted again and the water redirected her footing so that the alignment failed once more, her weight transferring sideways without correction and the connection stretching further.

He felt the change immediately, the increase in tension moving through his arm as her balance shifted beyond what his position could fully counter, and he adjusted his stance again, though there was little left to adjust, his feet already placed at the edge of what the floor could offer, his body working to maintain a hold that no longer had a stable point to draw toward. Their hands remained joined, but the connection had begun to change, the grip tightening beyond comfort, the pressure between their fingers increasing as the strain grew, the contact no longer neutral but a point at which force accumulated without release, the skin compressed, the joints adjusting under load, the connection bearing more than it had been meant to carry.

He pulled again, the effort complete and the result unchanged, her body moving toward him for a fraction before shifting away again as the path between them broke under the movement of water beneath her feet, the distance widening further, not dramatically but enough that the strain increased beyond what could be sustained without consequence. The first loss did not come as silence but as absence within sound, as he spoke again and felt the word form and leave him but did not hear it arrive, and she answered and he saw the movement of her lips and the shape of the reply without receiving the sound in a way that could be held, the exchange of words not stopping but failing to cross.

Their hands remained joined, the connection holding even as the words between them no longer did, the second loss following as reduction rather than break, what could be heard diminishing so that fragments no longer carried full meaning, a name becoming only a sound, a phrase becoming only motion without clear content, the effort to speak remaining even as the ability to transmit what was spoken continued to diminish. He tried again and she tried again, the effort remaining while the result did not, until the third loss arrived as the moment in which even the attempt to speak no longer held its previous function, their mouths moving while the words ceased to be the primary way meaning traveled between them, the connection in their hands carrying more than anything they could say, the pressure between their fingers communicating urgency, presence, direction, and the shared recognition that what had been spoken before would not be spoken again in the same way.

The water moved again, the floor shifted again, the alignment broke again, and their hands held as the space between them widened beyond what the connection could overcome, the grip adjusting under the strain as their fingers tightened further and then shifted when the pressure exceeded what the position could maintain, the contact not breaking at once but reducing, the surface between their hands decreasing as the force within it increased. He did not release and she did not let go, but the connection no longer occupied the same space, the water carrying her footing further away, the angle between them increasing, the tension reaching its limit as their fingers held at the edge of contact, the pressure concentrated into a smaller point while the rest of the grip gave way, the connection reduced to the last place where force could still be carried before it slipped—not suddenly and not all at once, but in a motion that completed itself once it began, their fingers losing contact not by choice but by the condition that had formed around them, the separation occurring as the force between them exceeded what the contact could sustain.

Her hand moved away while his remained where it had been, the shape of the grip staying in his fingers even after the contact was gone, the space between them remaining no longer crossed as the water continued to move, the radio continued to speak, the rain continued against the roof, and the last words spoken did not remain as words but as the moment in which they could no longer be heard.

PART II

The Ones Who Could Not Act

STORY 5

The Window

BEFORE THE GLASS BECAME something that could break, it had functioned as a boundary that did not require attention, a surface that separated inside from outside without appearing to do so. It allowed light to pass through without distortion, held back air without being felt, and framed the world beyond the house in a way that made it appear contained, ordered, and at a distance that could be observed without consequence. The window did not announce itself. It existed as part of the wall, part of the structure, part of the expectation that what was outside would remain outside.

The room in which it was set faced the side yard, its view angled just enough that the street could be seen without being central. The glass extended from a few inches above the floor to a height that allowed a person standing within the room to look outward without bending or reaching, the frame dividing it into sections that had once been necessary for construction but now served only to organize the view. The sill held small objects that had been placed there over time and left without intention to remove them: a folded paper, a small plant in a pot that had been turned periodically to catch the light, a book that had been set down and not returned to its shelf.

Outside, the yard sloped slightly away from the house, the ground uneven in ways that had settled over years of weather and use. The fence at the edge of the property marked a boundary that had once been clear but now held gaps where boards had shifted or warped, the line of it visible more by habit than by precision. Beyond it, another yard continued, then another, the sequence of properties extending toward the line of trees that marked where the land dropped toward the creek.

The sky held a color that suggested change without defining it, a flattening of light that reduced contrast and made distance harder to judge. The trees beyond the fence moved slightly, their branches shifting in patterns that did not yet form a single direction. Leaves turned and settled, then turned again, catching the light differently each time, the movement repetitive but not yet forceful enough to demand attention.

Inside, the room held its usual arrangement. The chair near the window faced outward, positioned not by design but by use, the angle of it allowing someone seated there to look through the glass without turning fully. A table stood to one side, its surface holding objects that had accumulated over time and remained because they had not yet been needed elsewhere. The air in the room remained still, the temperature unchanged, the sense of enclosure intact.

He stood near the window without touching it, his position close enough that he could see the details beyond the glass clearly, but not so close that his reflection interfered with the view. His attention rested outward, not fixed on any one point, but moving across the yard, the fence, the neighboring structures, the line of trees beyond. The scene remained continuous, unbroken, the window allowing it to be taken in without interruption.

The radio in the other room carried into this one faintly, its voice indistinct but present, the rhythm of speech marking that information continued to be given even when it was not fully heard. The tone remained steady, procedural, the cadence of updates delivered in a manner that suggested continuity rather than urgency. The words did not yet alter the room.

A shift in the air outside moved across the yard, visible first in the way the grass bent, then in the way the branches of the trees aligned more consistently in one direction. The movement did not increase immediately in force, but it gained coherence, the separate motions of leaves and limbs beginning to follow a shared pattern. The sky held its color, but the light beneath it changed again, flattening further, reducing depth in a way that made objects appear closer and less distinct at the same time.

He placed his hand on the back of the chair without sitting, the contact brief, not an action but a point of balance as his attention remained on what he could see through the glass. The window held its clarity. The boundary remained intact. The world beyond it continued to appear as something observed rather than something that could enter.

The first sound that differed from the rest did not come from within the room. It came from outside, a loose object striking against something fixed, the impact carrying across the yard and reaching the house with enough force to be heard distinctly. The sound did not repeat immediately. It remained singular, separate from the continuous movement of wind and the steady presence of rain that had begun to fall lightly against the roof.

He did not move away from the window. His attention shifted slightly, narrowing toward the direction from which the sound had come, but the view itself did not yet provide confirmation of what had caused it. The yard remained visible. The fence remained in place. The objects within sight had not yet rearranged themselves in a way that could be identified as change.

The rain increased gradually, the sound of it becoming more present against the roof and against the glass, the individual impacts merging into a continuous texture that filled the space between interior and exterior. The window carried that sound without transmitting the movement itself, the surface holding firm, the barrier remaining complete.

A second impact followed, closer this time, the sound sharper, the direction more immediate. The air outside moved more forcefully now, the branches of the trees bending further, the leaves no longer shifting but driven, the pattern of motion no longer varied but aligned. The yard changed in the way it held movement, the ground no longer appearing still beneath the air that moved over it.

He stepped closer to the window then, reducing the distance between himself and the glass, his reflection beginning to appear faintly over the view beyond. The boundary remained clear. The interior held. The exterior moved. The separation between them continued to exist as something that did not require defense.

The rain struck the glass more directly now, the angle of it changed by the wind, the impacts visible as streaks that moved across the surface rather than falling straight downward. The window held them all, the water gathering and sliding away, the glass remaining intact, its function unchanged.

Another object moved across the yard, this one visible, low and fast, carried by the wind in a path that did not follow the contours of the ground. It struck the fence, lodged briefly, then shifted again as the force against it increased. The movement did not yet alter the structure of the yard, but it marked a change in how objects within it behaved.

He raised his hand slightly, not yet touching the glass, but close enough that the distance between his skin and the surface could be measured without contact. The window remained unchanged. The boundary held. The separation between what could be seen and what could be felt remained intact.

Behind him, the radio voice rose slightly, its cadence tightening, the words no longer spaced but layered more closely together. The tone remained controlled, but the structure of the information had shifted, the updates no longer framed as possibility but as progression.

The wind increased again, the movement outside no longer intermittent but sustained, the branches of the trees bending in a single direction, the fence shifting slightly under the pressure, the yard no longer appearing as a stable surface but as something acted upon continuously.

He placed his hand against the glass.

The contact was immediate, the surface cool beneath his palm, the boundary now not only seen but felt. The window did not move. It did not respond. It held.

For the moment.

And what it held remained on the other side.

The contact of his hand against the glass did not change the window, but it changed how he occupied the space in relation to it, the boundary no longer only observed but measured through the pressure of his palm against its surface. The glass remained firm, its resistance complete, the separation between inside and outside still intact even as the movement beyond it increased. What had earlier been a view now became something encountered, the distance between him and what he saw reduced to the thickness of the pane.

Outside, the wind no longer moved in intervals. It held. The branches of the trees bent in a sustained direction, their motion no longer returning to stillness between gusts. Leaves tore free and traveled across the yard in paths that did not follow the ground, rising and dropping in irregular arcs before striking against the fence or the side of the house. The rain, carried at an angle, struck the glass with a force that made each impact visible, the surface marked by continuous motion that did not settle before the next contact occurred.

The window carried all of it without yielding, the water spreading across its surface and running downward in uneven lines, the glass distorting the view only slightly where the movement of water crossed it. The frame held steady, the divisions within it organizing the shifting scene into sections that made the movement appear contained even when it was not.

He pressed his hand more firmly against the glass, not to test its strength but to confirm its presence, the boundary remaining constant under increased pressure. The coolness of it held against his skin, unchanged by the movement beyond it, the interior of the room maintaining its stillness even as the exterior continued to reorganize itself.

Behind him, the radio voice rose again, the cadence tightening further, the repetition of locations and instructions forming a sequence that no longer allowed for delay. The words entered the room with more insistence, no longer part of the background, but not yet something he turned toward. His attention remained fixed outward, the window holding his focus as the point at which the changing world could still be understood without being entered.

A larger object moved into view from the right side of the yard, carried by the wind at a height that did not align with the ground. It rotated as it traveled, its shape difficult to identify until it struck the fence and broke apart, the pieces separating and moving in different directions, some falling, others lifted again by the continued force of the air. The yard did not absorb the movement. It transmitted it.

The fence shifted again, more visibly now, the boards bending inward and then returning, not fully to their original position, but enough to maintain their line. The structure held, but not without movement, the boundary it represented no longer fixed in place but responsive to the force against it.

The rain intensified, the sound against the glass deepening, the individual impacts merging into a continuous pressure that filled the space between interior and exterior. The window did not transmit the force, but it carried its presence, the vibration of impact registering faintly through the surface where his hand remained.

He did not remove his hand.

The contact anchored him to the boundary, the position holding his attention even as the scene beyond it became more difficult to interpret in discrete terms. Objects no longer moved independently. They moved within the same force, their paths intersecting, their motion overlapping in ways that made it harder to distinguish one from another.

Another impact struck the side of the house, closer than before, the sound sharper, the direction more immediate. The window did not move in response, but the awareness of proximity altered the way the space was held, the distance between what could be seen and what could be felt narrowing.

He shifted his weight slightly, not stepping back, but adjusting his stance to remain balanced as the sound continued around him. The room behind him remained unchanged. The air within it still held. The objects within it remained where they had been placed. The boundary at the glass continued to define the limit between movement and stillness.

The radio voice broke through more clearly for a moment, the words forming a complete instruction that reached him without interruption, something about leaving, about moving to higher ground, about not waiting. The sentence held long enough to be understood, then dissolved again into the continuous flow of updates.

He did not turn.

Outside, the movement intensified again, the wind driving the rain more forcefully against the glass, the angle of impact shifting so that the water no longer moved only downward, but across, the surface of the window marked by intersecting lines that did not settle before being replaced. The visibility through the glass reduced slightly, not obscured, but altered, the clarity of the view broken by the continuous motion across it.

The frame of the window held, its edges defining the space through which the exterior could be seen, the divisions within it still intact, though the movement within those divisions no longer appeared contained. The yard beyond no longer held its previous shape. The ground remained, but what moved across it did not follow its contours.

He lifted his hand from the glass briefly, not removing it entirely, but breaking the contact for a moment before placing it back again, the motion small but deliberate, as if confirming that the boundary remained where he had found it. The surface met his hand again with the same resistance, the same coolness, the same unyielding presence.

Another object struck the glass.

Not directly in front of him, but close enough that the impact registered through both sound and vibration, the force carried across the surface in a way that reached his hand before it reached his ears. The glass held. The object fell away.

The boundary remained intact.

But the distance between impact and contact had narrowed.

He kept his hand where it was.

The window held.

And what moved beyond it pressed closer.

The impact did not break the glass, but it altered the relationship between what the window held and what pressed against it, the boundary no longer existing as something assumed but as something tested. The surface beneath his hand remained firm, yet the knowledge of its exposure changed how he understood the space, the distance between interior and exterior reduced not by measurement but by pressure.

Outside, the wind carried more than movement now. It carried force with direction, the paths of objects no longer incidental but driven,the air itself functioning as something that transported weight rather than merely displacing it. Debris crossed the yard at varying heights, some pieces sliding along the ground, others lifted and thrown, their trajectories intersecting in ways that did not allow for prediction.

The rain struck the glass with sustained intensity, the surface marked continuously by the contact, the lines of water no longer forming and clearing but remaining in motion without pause. The view through the window shifted from clarity to distortion, not obscured entirely, but altered enough that distance became uncertain, the position of objects harder to fix within the frame.

He kept his hand against the glass, the contact now registering more than temperature, the faint vibration of impact traveling through the surface into his palm, each strike carried not as a single event but as part of a continuous field of pressure. The window did not yield, but it no longer appeared separate from what acted upon it.

Another object moved into view, larger than the ones before, its motion less erratic and more direct, carried by the wind in a path that aligned with the face of the house. It struck the fence and did not break apart, the structure absorbing part of the force while transmitting the rest, the boards bending further than before before returning unevenly to their line. The fence did not fail, but it did not remain unchanged, and the yard between the fence and the house no longer held empty space, having become a channel through which movement passed, the ground beneath it still visible but no longer stable in the way it had been earlier, the distinction between object and force blurring so that the movement of one could no longer be separated from the other.

Behind him, the radio voice continued, its cadence now urgent enough that the words pressed into the room whether they were received or not, instructions repeating without pause, locations named again and again, the structure of the message no longer allowing for interpretation, the tone remaining controlled while the spacing between phrases closed so that the voice filled the space in a way that competed with the sound of the storm itself. He did not turn, his attention remaining fixed on the window, the boundary now carrying more meaning than the information behind him, the glass holding his focus as the point at which everything converged, the interior still defined by its separation, the exterior pressing against that separation with increasing force.

The frame of the window began to register movement, not visible at first but perceptible in the way the glass responded to impact, the surface flexing slightly within its setting, the vibration no longer dissipating immediately. The structure held, but it held under strain, and he pressed his hand more firmly against the glass, the contact anchoring him as the movement beyond intensified, the boundary now something he could feel as well as see, the coolness of the surface remaining while the steadiness of it changed, the resistance no longer absolute but responsive.

Another impact struck closer to where his hand rested, the sound sharp, the force transmitted directly through the pane, the glass holding but the vibration remaining longer this time, the surface carrying the energy of the strike before releasing it, while the yard shifted again not in its form but in how it behaved, the movement within it no longer separate events but a continuous field in which objects moved without clear origin or destination, their paths overlapping, their timing unpredictable.

He lifted his hand slightly, then placed it back again, the motion deliberate, as if confirming that the boundary remained where it had been, the glass meeting his hand again with resistance though the sensation had changed, the surface no longer entirely still beneath his touch as the rain intensified further, the sound against the window deepening into a constant pressure that filled the space between inside and outside, the visibility through the glass reducing again as distortion increased, the lines of water crossing in patterns that did not clear before being replaced.

The frame creaked, a sound not from impact but from strain, the structure adjusting to the force applied from the outside, the movement slight but no longer absent, and he heard it and did not move as another object struck the glass closer, the impact sharper, the vibration immediate, the glass holding but not without response as a line appeared—not a break, not yet, but something within the surface that had not been there before—and he kept his hand against it, felt the difference, as the boundary remained and yet had begun to change.

The line in the glass did not widen immediately, but it altered everything that followed, the boundary no longer functioning as something assumed or even simply tested, but as something already in the process of giving way. The surface beneath his hand still held, yet the knowledge of what had begun within it changed how the space could be occupied, the separation between inside and outside no longer complete even where it remained unbroken.

The wind continued to drive against the house without pause, the force sustained rather than arriving in intervals, the objects carried within it moving in paths that now aligned more directly with the window itself. The yard no longer contained the motion passing through it. It directed it, the ground beneath no longer a resting place but a channel, the fence beyond bending again under pressure that did not release long enough for it to return fully to its previous position.

The rain struck the glass with increasing force, the impacts merging into a continuous pressure that no longer allowed the surface to return to stillness between contacts. Water moved across the pane in overlapping lines, distorting what could be seen beyond it, the clarity of the view reduced to shifting fragments that did not hold long enough to be fully recognized.

He kept his hand against the glass, though the sensation beneath it had changed, the faint vibration no longer dissipating cleanly, the surface responding with a subtle movement that had not been present before. The boundary remained, but it no longer felt fixed, the resistance altered by the strain now carried within it.

Another object struck the window.

Closer.

Harder.

The impact did not shatter the glass, but the line within it extended, not quickly, but with a clarity that could not be mistaken, the fracture traveling across the surface in a path that followed the pressure applied to it. The glass held, but it held differently, the integrity of it no longer uniform, the surface divided by what had begun to open within it.

He felt the change through his hand before he fully saw it, the shift in the way the glass carried the force of impact reaching him through contact, the vibration no longer dispersed evenly but redirected along the line that had formed. The boundary did not break.

But it had begun to fail.

Behind him, the radio voice continued, the cadence urgent now, the repetition of instruction constant, the words pressing into the room without pause. He did not turn toward it. The information remained secondary to the condition at the window, the point at which everything converged still holding his attention fully.

The frame creaked again, louder this time, the sound carrying through the wall and into the space around him, the structure adjusting under the sustained force from outside. The movement remained slight, but it was no longer subtle, the strain now audible as well as felt.

The wind drove another object across the yard, this one larger, its path direct, its movement not interrupted by the ground before it reached the house. It struck the glass at an angle, the impact sharp, the force carried through the surface in a way that caused the fracture to spread further, the line branching into smaller lines that extended outward from it.

The glass did not shatter.

But it changed again.

The surface beneath his hand no longer felt uniform, the difference between intact and fractured areas perceptible through touch, the resistance uneven, the vibration following paths that did not align with the structure of the pane as it had before.

He did not remove his hand.

The contact anchored him to the boundary even as it altered, the position holding his attention as the distinction between inside and outside narrowed further. The window still held, but what it held had begun to enter it.

Another impact followed.

Then another.

The intervals between them shortened, the surface no longer returning to stillness between strikes, the strain carried continuously across the pane. The fracture lines extended incrementally with each contact, not explosively, but with a steady progression that could not be reversed.

The view beyond the glass no longer held coherence. The yard, the fence, the trees—everything that had once been distinct now moved within the same field of distortion, the lines of water across the pane intersecting with the fractures beneath them, the image broken into shifting segments that did not align.

He pressed his hand more firmly against the glass, not to stop what was happening, but to remain connected to it, the boundary now something that could be felt changing in real time. The surface responded under his palm, the resistance no longer absolute, the movement within it subtle but undeniable.

The frame shifted again, the sound of it no longer intermittent, but sustained, the structure adjusting continuously under the pressure applied to it. The wall around the window held, but the point at which it met the frame had begun to register strain.

The next impact did not come from an object.

It came from the wind itself.

The force struck the house in a sustained movement, the pressure carried across the surface of the window without interruption, the glass bowing slightly within the frame, the fracture lines responding to the shift by extending further.

He felt it.

Did not move.

The boundary remained.

But it no longer separated in the same way.

The glass held.

But only as something already in the process of breaking.

You're right—the ending loosened into fragmented cadence again. This is exactly where you want one continuous pressure line, not stepped release.

The glass did not shatter all at once. It held in its brokenness, the fractures spreading across its surface until the pane no longer functioned as a single thing, the boundary divided into sections that remained in place even as their integrity failed, the line that had first appeared multiplying and branching outward until no part of the glass remained untouched, the surface held together not by strength but by the frame that contained it.

His hand remained against it, the contact changing beneath his palm, the resistance uneven now, the surface no longer smooth but carrying the subtle shifts of pieces that had begun to separate without yet falling, the vibration of each impact no longer traveling cleanly through the pane but breaking along the fractures, redirected, absorbed, and returned in ways that no longer aligned with what had come before.

Outside, the wind continued without interruption, the force sustained, the movement of objects no longer distinct from the movement of the air itself, the yard no longer functioning as a space that held things but as a passage through which motion traveled without settling, the fence bending again and again without returning fully to its original position between strikes, while the rain struck the glass as part of that same force, no longer falling but driven, the impacts continuous, the surface marked by intersecting lines of water that followed and crossed the fractures beneath them so that the view beyond disappeared as something that could be understood, replaced by shifting patterns of distortion that did not resolve into recognizable forms.

He did not remove his hand, the boundary remaining where it had been but no longer holding what it had held, the distinction between inside and outside narrowed to the thickness of the fractured glass, and even that thickness beginning to fail as the pressure against it increased. Another impact struck, then another, the glass not breaking apart but yielding, not through pieces falling away but through the way it gave under the force applied to it, the pane bowing further within the frame, the fractures widening enough to allow movement between what had been separated, the resistance that had once held firm across its entire surface now existing only in segments, each section responding differently under strain.

He felt the change immediately, the surface beneath his hand shifting not as a single plane but as many, the alignment altered, the contact no longer stable, the boundary not disappearing but no longer functioning, while behind him the radio voice continued, the words no longer distinguishable as separate phrases, the cadence compressed into a continuous stream that filled the room without resolving into meaning, the sound still present but no longer carrying what it once had.

The next force did not arrive as a discrete impact but as continuation, the wind pressing against the house without pause, the pressure sustained long enough that the glass could not return to stillness between movements, the fractures responding as the lines widened incrementally, the segments shifting against one another within the frame while he kept his hand where it was, the contact now carrying motion as the glass beneath his palm moved, slightly but enough.

The first piece gave way not from the center but near the edge, a small section separating from the rest, the bond that had held it failing under accumulated strain, the piece not falling immediately but shifting, remaining for a moment, then dropping inward as the air entered—not as a rush but as presence—the boundary opening at a single point, the separation between inside and outside no longer complete.

He did not step back, the opening remaining small but not closing, another section shifting, then another, the fractures widening, the segments loosening, the structure of the pane continuing to hold while the surface no longer functioned as a barrier, the air moving through the gaps now, carrying with it the force that had been held outside so that the movement was no longer limited to what could be seen but entered the space where he stood, the temperature changing, the pressure changing, the sound changing, the room no longer holding in the same way.

He removed his hand not abruptly but because there was no longer a surface that held it in the same form, the glass continuing to give, not collapsing but opening, the pieces remaining where they could and falling where they could not, the frame holding while what it contained no longer did, the window remaining but no longer separating, and what had been held outside entering without needing to break all at once.

STORY 6

The Other Side of the Wall

Before the wall became something that divided more than space, it existed as part of the structure that allowed the house to hold its shape without being noticed, a surface that separated rooms without requiring attention, carrying weight, containing sound, and marking boundaries that did not need to be tested in order to be trusted. It stood between spaces that had been assigned different purposes, the kitchen on one side, the back room on the other, its presence felt only in the way movement changed when passing through the doorway cut into it, the body adjusting without thought as it crossed from one arrangement into another.

The wall carried the quiet accumulation of use, the marks of contact softened by time, a place where a chair had once rested too close, leaving a faint impression in the paint, where hands had brushed against it at the turn of the doorway, the surface dulled slightly at that point without appearing worn from a distance, and where a small nail had been driven into it years earlier to hold something that no longer hung there, the hole left behind too minor to repair and too small to notice unless the light struck it at an angle. Nothing about the wall suggested importance, and it held because it had always held.

On one side, the kitchen remained ordered according to repetition, the placement of objects determined less by design than by habit, the counter holding what had been used most recently while the cabinets contained what had not, the table standing near the window with its surface cleared and filled again over time without settling into a fixed arrangement, and the chairs positioned around it not evenly but in the way they had last been left. The room carried the sounds of use even when no one moved within it, the faint hum of appliances, the occasional shift of air through the vents, and the subtle movement of the structure responding to changes in temperature.

On the other side, the back room held a different rhythm, less defined by sequence and more by accumulation, the objects within it arranged according to need rather than repetition, items placed where they had been used last rather than where they belonged. The floor held more than the kitchen floor did, boxes set against the wall, a chair turned slightly away from the table it had once been part of, and a shelf that carried things not used daily but not stored away entirely, the room not resisting disorder but containing it.

The doorway between them allowed movement without interruption, the frame wide enough that carrying something through it did not require adjustment unless what was carried extended beyond the body's usual width, the threshold not rising and not marking a change in level, existing only as the point at which one room became another. He moved through that doorway without thinking, carrying a small object from one side to the other and placing it down without remembering the act of carrying it once it had been set in place, the movement belonging to the category of actions that did not require attention, the body completing them while the mind remained elsewhere.

The radio sat on the counter in the kitchen, its volume low, the voice steady, the words entering the room without altering it, locations named, conditions described, and instructions given in a tone that suggested continuity rather than interruption, the cadence consistent enough that it did not yet demand full attention. The information existed within the space, but it did not yet define it.

Outside, the weather had begun to change in ways that were visible but not yet decisive, the light flattening, the air carrying a pressure that did not yet translate into force, and the trees beyond the house moving in patterns that did not align fully but no longer remained still. The yard held its shape, the fence stood in place, and the ground had not yet begun to move.

He paused in the kitchen, his hand resting briefly against the counter, his attention moving outward without settling on any one point, the window drawing his gaze without holding it, while the wall beside him remained what it had always been, a surface that contained the space, a boundary that did not require interpretation.

From the other side of it came a sound, not loud and not sudden, but distinct, the kind of sound that did not belong to the usual pattern of the room, and he turned his head slightly, not fully, just enough to register the direction from which it had come, the wall marking that direction without revealing what lay beyond it. The sound did not repeat immediately, remaining singular and separate from the rest of what the house carried, and he did not move toward it yet, the wall holding, the rooms remaining divided, and whatever had caused the sound not crossing through.

The radio continued, its voice steady, the words still forming a sequence that could be followed if attention were given to them, and he did not turn it off or turn it up, allowing it to remain where it was, part of the room without yet becoming central to it, while another sound followed, closer this time, or perhaps clearer, the difference difficult to determine. The wall did not change or shift or allow what lay beyond it to be seen, remaining a surface, a boundary, a structure that held.

He stepped toward it then, not quickly and not slowly, but with a movement that acknowledged the presence of something that had not been there before, the distance between where he stood and where the wall began closing without resistance, the floor beneath him unchanged and the air within the room still holding, and he stopped a short distance from it, close enough that the wall occupied his full attention but not close enough to touch. The surface remained still, the paint unbroken, the marks of use unchanged, nothing in its appearance indicating difference, and yet the sound had come from beyond it, and the space on the other side no longer held the same certainty it had before.

He raised his hand slightly, not yet placing it against the wall but holding it in the space just before contact, as if the boundary might be measured without being touched, and the wall remained while what lay beyond it did not show, whatever had begun on the other side not yet crossing through but having been heard, and in that hearing the division no longer held in the same way it had before.

His hand did not touch the wall immediately, the distance between his palm and the surface held for a moment as if the boundary might be understood without contact, as if what had been heard could remain contained on the other side so long as it was not engaged directly, the wall standing as it had before, its surface unbroken, its structure unchanged, the separation between the rooms still intact even as the certainty of that separation had begun to shift.

The sound did not repeat in the same form, but it did not disappear either, its presence continuing in a way that did not resolve into a single identifiable source, something within the space beyond the wall carrying movement that did not align with the usual pattern of the back room, not loud enough to be called impact, not continuous enough to be called motion, but present, and in its presence altering how the wall could be regarded.

He closed the remaining distance and placed his hand against the surface, the contact immediate and complete, the paint cool beneath his palm, the structure beneath it firm, the boundary registering as solid in the way it had always been, nothing moving in response and nothing giving, and yet the sound continuing, not clearly through the wall and not entirely around it, but distributed in a way that resisted precise location, the wall not transmitting it cleanly but not fully blocking it either, altering it.

He pressed his hand more firmly against the surface, not to push through it but to feel whether what lay beyond might register as pressure, whether the boundary that held visually might carry some indication of change through contact, and while the wall did not respond with visible movement, the sensation beneath his hand was no longer entirely neutral, the surface carrying a faint irregularity that had not been present before, not a difference in structure but in how it was being held.

Behind him, the radio voice continued, the cadence tightening, the repetition of instructions more frequent, the tone still controlled but no longer distant, the words entering the room with more insistence without redirecting his attention, the wall holding it fully, the boundary now the point at which everything converged.

Another sound followed, closer or perhaps stronger, the distinction between those two no longer holding, the change registering not as location or volume but as reduction in separation, the space between him and its source feeling altered without being measured. He shifted his hand slightly along the surface, not removing it but moving it laterally as if searching for a point at which the difference beneath it might become more defined, his palm gliding across the paint while maintaining continuous contact, the wall remaining smooth, the marks of use unchanged, the structure holding without visible strain.

Yet the sensation followed, not precisely but enough, and he paused with his hand still against the wall, his body aligned toward it as the rest of the room receded in importance, the sounds behind him continuing without carrying weight, the boundary remaining in place while no longer holding its previous certainty, what lay beyond it beginning to register within it, not as something visible and not as something measurable, but as something that could not be ignored.

The sound shifted again, this time not as a single instance but as a brief sequence, two movements in close succession, the pattern not regular and not repeating, but no longer singular, the wall not moving in response and the surface beneath his hand not breaking or giving, yet the presence beyond it no longer appearing isolated. He leaned slightly closer, not enough to press his body against the wall but enough to reduce the distance further, his attention narrowing as the space around him diminished and the boundary took on more weight, the room behind him remaining unchanged while its relevance diminished.

Another sound came, not sharper but more sustained, not striking and disappearing but carrying, and the wall remained intact while no longer feeling still, prompting him to adjust his stance, placing more of his weight forward not to push but to remain aligned with what he was sensing, his hand still against the surface, his fingers spreading slightly as if increasing contact might clarify what lay beyond, the surface beneath his palm holding while the sensation within it shifted, not movement exactly but the absence of stillness.

Behind him, the radio voice rose again, the words now clearly instructive, the cadence compressed, the message continuous, but he did not turn toward it, the information existing without intersecting with what was happening at the wall as the sound came again, now accompanied not by a second sound but by a change in pressure, faint but present, felt through his hand as a difference in the way the wall resisted his touch, the surface no longer entirely independent of what lay beyond it, the boundary remaining while no longer functioning as a complete separation, and he did not remove his hand because the contact had become necessary, the wall holding even as what was on the other side had begun to press back.

The pressure did not arrive as force in the way impact had earlier been imagined, but as a change in how the wall held itself, the resistance beneath his hand no longer uniform, the surface no longer entirely independent of what lay beyond it. The structure remained intact, the paint unbroken, the line of the wall unchanged, yet the sensation carried through it altered in a way that could not be separated from the presence on the other side, the boundary still visible as solid while no longer functioning as absolute.

He did not remove his hand, the contact now serving as the only point at which the change could be measured, his palm remaining flat against the surface while his fingers adjusted slightly to increase the area of contact, the pressure beneath them not pushing outward but altering the balance of what had previously held steady. The wall did not move in any way that could be seen, but it no longer felt still.

The sound continued, not as isolated instances but as a pattern that refused to settle into repetition, each occurrence similar enough to the last to suggest continuity but different enough to prevent it from becoming predictable, the space beyond the wall no longer holding discrete events but carrying something that remained in motion without resolving into a fixed form. The wall altered that motion as it passed through, not transmitting it clearly and not fully blocking it, but reshaping it into something that could be sensed without being located.

Behind him, the radio voice persisted, the cadence now compressed into a continuous stream of instruction, the tone controlled but insistent, the spacing between phrases reduced to the point that the words overlapped in their delivery. He did not turn toward it, the information no longer competing for his attention, the wall holding it entirely, the boundary now the point at which everything converged.

He leaned closer, reducing the distance between his body and the surface without yet placing his full weight against it, the alignment of his posture narrowing around the contact point, the rest of the room receding further in relevance. The air behind him remained still, the objects within it unchanged, but none of it held the same importance as what was registering through the wall.

The pressure shifted again, not increasing in magnitude but in distribution, the area beneath his hand no longer carrying the same response across its surface, certain points registering more distinctly than others, the sensation uneven, as if what lay beyond was no longer aligned evenly against the structure. The wall did not bow. It did not flex visibly. Yet the way it resisted his touch had changed.

He moved his hand slightly, not lifting it, but sliding it across the paint to follow where the sensation seemed strongest, his palm maintaining contact as his fingers traced the surface, searching not for a break but for a point of clarity within what had become diffuse. The wall remained smooth, the marks of use unchanged, the structure holding without visible sign of failure, and yet the sensation did not dissipate when he moved. It followed.

Not precisely.

But enough.

He stopped, his hand pressed flat again, his fingers spread, his attention narrowed completely to the contact point, the rest of the space around him no longer holding significance. The sound came again, not louder, but more sustained, the movement beyond the wall carrying through in a way that suggested continuity rather than interruption.

Then something changed.

Not in the sound.

Not in the visible structure.

But in the way the wall responded.

The pressure did not push outward, but it settled inward, the resistance beneath his hand decreasing at a single point, not enough to be seen, but enough to be felt, the surface no longer offering the same solidity across its full area. The difference was slight.

But it was not imagined.

He pressed more firmly at that point, not to force it, but to confirm it, his palm adjusting so that more of his weight aligned with the change he had detected. The wall did not give.

But it did not hold in the same way.

Behind him, the radio voice rose again, the instructions now urgent, the cadence no longer spaced but continuous, the words pressing into the room without pause. He did not turn. The information existed, but it did not intersect with what he was experiencing at the wall.

The sound came again.

And this time it carried something else.

Not volume.

Not direction.

But duration.

It remained longer.

The pressure beneath his hand responded to it, the difference at that single point becoming more defined, the surface no longer evenly resistant, the structure still intact but no longer uniform.

He did not move his hand away.

The contact had become necessary.

The boundary remained.

But it no longer held as one.

The difference beneath his hand did not widen immediately, but it did not return to what it had been, the single point at which the wall no longer resisted evenly remaining present as something that could be felt even when the rest of the surface held its usual firmness, the structure still appearing intact, the paint unbroken, the line of the wall unchanged, yet the continuity of it interrupted in a way that could not be seen but could not be dismissed, the boundary no longer functioning as a single, uniform plane.

He adjusted his stance, bringing more of his weight forward not to push against the wall but to remain aligned with the point where the difference had emerged, his palm still flat, his fingers spread to increase contact, the sensation beneath them no longer diffuse but gathering, the area of reduced resistance becoming more defined through continued contact while the wall did not move outward or shift visibly, but no longer held in the same way.

The sound from beyond the wall continued, no longer arriving as isolated instances but as a sustained presence, the movement behind the structure carrying through in a pattern that did not resolve into repetition, the intervals between sounds collapsing into continuity while the wall altered that presence as it passed through, not allowing it to arrive clearly but no longer fully containing it, and behind him the radio voice persisted, its cadence now urgent, the instructions repeated without pause, the tone controlled but no longer distant, the words entering the room in a continuous stream that did not wait to be received, yet he did not turn because the wall held his attention completely.

He pressed more firmly at the point where the resistance had changed, not striking and not forcing but applying sustained pressure as if the boundary might reveal more through contact than through observation, and the surface responded differently there, not yielding in a way that could be called movement but no longer offering the same resistance as the rest of the wall, the difference slight but increasing, not quickly and not dramatically but enough, the shift carried through the center of his palm as the pressure redistributed and the structure beneath it no longer held evenly, the boundary beginning to respond in a way that could not be separated from what lay beyond it.

He moved his hand slightly, testing the edges of the change, sliding his palm outward from the center point and then back again, confirming that the difference remained localized but no longer fixed, the area of altered resistance expanding by a fraction that could be tracked only through touch while the wall still appeared unchanged even as it no longer behaved as it had, and the sound shifted again, not louder and not closer but more continuous, the movement behind the wall no longer breaking into separate instances, the presence sustained long enough that it altered the timing of everything else within the room so that the air on his side remained still but the stillness had lost its certainty.

He leaned closer, his shoulder nearing the surface, his body aligned fully with the point of change, the rest of the room receding completely in importance, the boundary now the only structure that held meaning, his hand remaining pressed flat, his fingers spread, the contact unbroken as the wall responded not outward and not with impact but inward, the surface beneath his hand giving slightly, the resistance decreasing in a way that could not be mistaken for variation, the structure shifting at that single point just enough to register as movement while the paint held and the surface remained intact but the material beneath it no longer fixed in place.

He did not pull away but pressed again, not harder but more deliberately, confirming the change as his palm followed the movement and the wall settled further, the difference no longer a point but an area, the boundary no longer uniform while behind him the radio voice continued, the words now indistinguishable as separate phrases, the cadence compressed into a continuous stream that filled the room without resolving into meaning, the sound existing without carrying significance.

The pressure from the other side increased, not as a strike but as sustained force, and the wall responded again as the surface beneath his hand shifted further inward, the resistance decreasing across a wider area, the structure no longer holding in the same alignment as a faint line appeared—not a crack, not yet, but a change in the surface marking where the pressure had begun to reorganize what had once been fixed—and he saw it and felt it and did not move as the boundary remained but had begun to open from the other side.

The line in the wall did not open suddenly, but it did not close again, the faint mark that had appeared remaining where it was, its presence altering the structure even as the surface still appeared intact, the paint holding across it unbroken to the eye while the continuity beneath had shifted so that the boundary no longer functioned as a single plane but as something that had begun to separate from within.

His hand remained pressed against the surface, the contact now carrying motion that had not been there before, the resistance beneath his palm uneven, the structure responding not as a whole but in parts, the difference spreading outward from the original point in a way that could be followed only through touch, the wall still standing without having failed yet no longer holding in the same way, the pressure from the other side arriving not as impact but as continuation, a sustained force that did not release long enough for the structure to recover, the movement beyond the wall no longer breaking into distinct events but remaining present, constant, and unresolved so that the sound itself became secondary, merging into the pressure as a single condition that could be felt even when it could not be clearly heard.

He adjusted his stance again without stepping back, bracing more fully against the floor, his body aligning with the point of contact, his arm no longer extended but engaged, the connection between his hand and the wall no longer passive as he did not push and did not withdraw, while the wall responded again and the surface beneath his palm shifted further inward, the resistance decreasing across a wider area as the faint line extended not sharply but with a slow clarity that followed the direction of pressure applied to it, the paint still holding while the structure beneath it separated, the boundary no longer fixed in place.

He felt the change before he saw it fully, the redistribution of pressure moving through his hand, the surface no longer supporting his touch in the same way, the alignment altered so that the contact itself became unstable, the wall not collapsing yet no longer resisting as it had, and behind him the radio voice continued, the words compressed into a continuous stream, the cadence no longer allowing distinction between phrases, the sound filling the room without resolving into meaning while he did not turn, its presence remaining but no longer intersecting with what was happening at the wall.

The line widened, not dramatically but enough, the surface beneath his hand giving further as resistance decreased to the point where the distinction between solid and not solid no longer held in the same way, the wall remaining upright and the structure still carrying its form while the boundary had begun to open from the inside, and he did not remove his hand because the contact had become the only way to measure what was changing as the surface shifted again, the movement beneath his palm no longer slight, the inward give more pronounced, the structure no longer able to hold evenly across the compromised area, the line extending further and branching slightly as separation beneath the paint spread outward in a pattern that followed the sustained pressure from the other side.

The first break did not come as collapse but as release, a small section of the wall giving inward not by falling away but by moving just enough to create space where there had been none, the surface dipping beneath his hand, the material beneath the paint no longer holding in place, the opening not immediately visible but fully present in what could be felt, and he pressed slightly at that point not to force it but to confirm it, his palm following the movement as the surface yielded further so that the boundary no longer resisted even minimal pressure at that location, the wall not falling yet having opened.

The pressure from the other side increased again not in force but in duration, the sustained presence continuing without interruption as the structure responded by giving further, the area of separation expanding and the surface no longer able to maintain alignment until the break became visible as a thin line where the paint separated and a narrow opening where the material beneath had shifted enough to allow space between what had once been joined, and he saw it and felt it and did not move as the opening did not widen immediately but did not close, the air changing not suddenly but distinctly, a difference in pressure, a difference in temperature, a difference in how the space held itself, the boundary having been crossed not by him but from the other side.

He removed his hand not abruptly but because there was no longer a surface that held it in the same way as the wall continued to give not by collapsing but by separating, the sections no longer fixed in a single plane, the structure holding its form while losing its function, the division between the rooms no longer complete, the opening remaining small but sufficient, the space beyond it no longer contained, the boundary no longer holding, and what had been on the other side entering without needing to break through all at once.

STORY 7

The Line That Didn't Reach

Before the line became something that failed to connect, it existed as part of a system that did not require attention, a simple extension of voice across distance, the instrument through which one room could reach another, one place could be carried into the next without movement of the body. It rested where it had been placed, its presence defined not by how it looked but by what it allowed, the quiet assurance that contact could be made when needed, that distance within the house could be crossed without effort.

The device sat on a small table near the wall, its position unchanged over time, the cord extending from it in a curve that had settled into the shape it was given, the line running along the baseboard before disappearing behind a piece of furniture and continuing into the structure beyond. The path of it was not followed, and it did not need to be, because its function did not depend on being seen in full but only on being available when called upon.

The room in which it stood held its usual order, the arrangement of objects determined by repetition, the surfaces cleared and filled according to use, the chair positioned near enough to the table that the device could be reached without standing, the air remaining still and the sounds within the room carrying without obstruction, including the quiet hum of appliances from another space, the faint movement of air through vents, and the structure of the house settling and adjusting in ways that did not interrupt the sense of enclosure.

He moved through the room without attention to the device, his actions directed elsewhere, his hands occupied with objects that required placement, his thoughts aligned with tasks that did not yet require interruption, while the line remained where it had been, its presence unchanged, its purpose intact without needing to be engaged.

Outside, the weather had begun to shift in ways that could be seen but not yet fully understood, the light flattening, the air carrying a pressure that suggested change without defining it, the trees beyond the window moving in patterns that did not yet align into force, the yard holding, the ground remaining stable, and the distinction between outside and inside continuing to hold.

The radio in another room carried into this one faintly, its voice steady, the cadence of information consistent, the words forming a sequence that could be followed without urgency, locations named, conditions described, and instructions given in a tone that suggested continuity rather than interruption, the sound remaining part of the environment, present but not central.

He passed by the table once, then again, his movement unbroken, the device remaining untouched, its presence neither ignored nor engaged, existing within the room as something that would be used when needed, not before, until the first indication that the line might be required came not from the device itself but from the change in the sound beyond the room, the wind rising outside, the movement against the house becoming more distinct, the rhythm of what lay beyond shifting from variation into direction while the radio voice altered slightly, its cadence tightening and the spacing between phrases shortening even as the tone remained controlled.

He paused then, not at the table but in the center of the room, his attention shifting without yet fixing on a single point, the awareness of change entering before the response to it had formed, the device remaining where it was, the line extending from it into the wall, its path unseen, its function still assumed to hold.

A sound came from outside, not loud but different, the kind of sound that suggested movement not contained within the usual pattern, and he turned slightly toward the window, his attention drawn outward while the room behind him held its shape, the objects within it unchanged, and the device still resting where it had been placed. The sound did not repeat immediately, but it remained, not as echo but as presence, while the radio voice continued, its words now more closely spaced, the sequence of information no longer separated by the same intervals as the message began to compress with the advancing conditions it described, and he did not move toward it, his attention remaining divided between what he could hear and what he could see.

Another sound followed, closer or perhaps clearer, the difference difficult to determine, and he turned then toward the table not quickly but with intention, the device remaining where it had always been, its surface unchanged, its form familiar, the line extending from it into the wall as it had before, the connection implied by its presence still assumed to hold. He stepped toward it, the distance closing without interruption, the floor beneath him unchanged and the air within the room still holding, his hand moving toward the device and stopping just above it as if the moment before contact might reveal whether the connection remained what it had been, the line not moving and not shifting, remaining what it appeared to be—a path, a connection, a way through—as he placed his hand on it and the room did not change even as the possibility of change had already entered through the space the line was meant to cross.

His hand rested on the device without lifting it immediately, the contact establishing presence before action as if the line might register intention before it was used, as if the connection it represented could be confirmed without being activated, the surface beneath his palm remaining unchanged, the weight familiar, the shape unchanged by the shift that had begun elsewhere in the house.

The sound outside continued, no longer in discrete intervals but as a growing condition, the wind carrying movement that did not return to stillness between gusts, the pressure against the structure increasing without announcing itself as force, while the radio voice persisted with a tightening cadence, instructions repeating with less space between them, the tone controlled but no longer distant as the words pressed into the room without requiring attention to be heard.

He lifted the device, the motion small and practiced, his hand aligning with its shape without adjustment as the receiver came away from its rest with a quiet, contained sound that did not alter anything beyond it, the line following and uncoiling slightly, its curve shifting as the connection extended from the table to his hand, the path of it still unseen beyond the wall but assumed to remain intact.

He brought it to his ear, the contact immediate, the expectation forming with it that the space within the receiver should hold sound, yet it did not, and the absence was not silence in the ordinary sense but a condition in which the expected presence of tone had failed to appear, the line offering nothing where something had always been, so he did not lower it and did not move but listened as the absence remained, carrying within it a faint irregularity that did not resolve into recognizable signal, the space within the receiver no longer neutral but not yet carrying meaning, the line failing to transmit what it had been meant to carry.

He adjusted his grip slightly, pressing the receiver more firmly against his ear as if contact might clarify what the connection could not, as if the distance between him and the device might be the source of interruption, the position changing while the result did not, and the sound outside continued to build, the movement against the house now sustained, the structure responding in subtle ways as the walls carried faint vibration that no longer remained absent, while the radio voice rose again with urgency, the cadence compressed into a continuous stream.

He did not turn toward it, the receiver holding his attention completely as he spoke, the word simple and placed clearly, directed into the space that had always carried it, and he heard himself but not through the line, the sound remaining within the room unreturned, the device offering no response, no acknowledgment, no indication that what had been sent had crossed the distance it was meant to bridge.

He waited, not long but long enough, the absence not resolving, and he spoke again with the same word, the same placement, the same intention, his voice steady and not yet shaped by urgency, the repetition an attempt to confirm what had not been received, yet the result did not change and the line did not carry, the faint irregularity within the receiver remaining, not increasing and not clarifying but present, the space within it occupied by something that did not function as sound.

He shifted the receiver slightly away from his ear, not lowering it fully but altering the angle as if position might reveal what contact could not, his gaze moving toward the cord where it extended from the base, following the line as far as it could be seen before it disappeared behind furniture and into the wall, the cord remaining still, not moving, not straining, not giving any indication that the connection it represented had changed, and he returned the receiver to his ear and listened again.

The absence held, but the disturbance within it seemed closer now, not in distance but in how it registered, the faint irregularity no longer entirely separate from the silence, the space within the receiver carrying something that had begun to form without yet becoming identifiable, and he spoke again, this time more than a single word but a phrase, the shape clear and the intention unchanged, the sound leaving him and not returning as the line remained extended between his hand and the wall, its path unchanged, its form intact, the connection still present in appearance yet not reaching across the distance it was meant to cross, not into whatever lay on the other side.

He held the receiver in place without lowering or replacing it, the attempt not ended but not succeeding, and the space between where he stood and where the line was meant to go no longer holding as something that could be crossed by voice alone.

The absence within the receiver did not remain empty, but it did not resolve into anything that could be called sound, the faint irregularity continuing to register in a way that suggested presence without clarity, the space within the device no longer neutral yet not carrying meaning that could be identified or understood, the line not returning his voice while what remained in its place had begun to change.

He kept the receiver against his ear, the contact steady, his hand holding it in position without adjustment as if movement might disrupt whatever was beginning to form within it, the connection no longer serving its intended purpose yet not severed, the cord extending from his hand to the base and into the wall, its path unchanged, its form intact, while what it carried had altered in a way that could not be seen.

The sound outside the house continued, the wind sustained, the movement against the structure no longer intermittent but constant, the pressure building without distinct intervals of release, while the radio voice behind him had become continuous, the cadence compressed, the words overlapping in a stream that no longer separated into individual instructions, and he did not turn toward it because the receiver held his attention completely as he listened, the irregularity within the line shifting not by increasing in volume and not by becoming clearer but by changing in structure, the disturbance no longer random but beginning to form a pattern that did not repeat yet did not dissipate, the presence within the receiver carrying a duration that extended beyond what silence would allow, not resembling voice yet no longer remaining apart from it.

He spoke again, not louder but more deliberately, placing the words into the receiver with care as if clarity on his end might produce clarity on the other, the phrase shaped fully and the intention unchanged, the sound leaving him and not returning as the line offered no acknowledgment, no confirmation, no interruption, yet the disturbance responded not as reply and not as echo but as alteration, the irregularity within the receiver shifting at the moment his voice entered it, the pattern changing in a way that aligned with the timing of his speech without forming words, the presence within the line no longer entirely independent of what he sent into it so that the connection did not carry his voice outward yet did not leave it untouched.

He held still, the receiver pressed against his ear, his body aligned with the device as the rest of the room receded further, the boundary of attention narrowing to the space within the line while the sound outside continued to build, the structure of the house responding in subtle vibrations, the walls carrying a faint movement that no longer remained absent, and he spoke again, a single word placed clearly, the disturbance shifting again more distinctly this time, not louder but closer to form, the pattern within the receiver altering at the moment of his voice so that the timing no longer remained incidental and the presence within the line reacted to what had been sent into it, not carrying it across distance but changing in relation to it.

He did not lower the receiver because the contact had become necessary, the line not reaching yet something within it beginning to answer, not in language and not in return but in response, and he listened more closely, adjusting the pressure of the receiver slightly against his ear without changing its position, increasing contact as if the difference might be clarified through proximity, the sound within remaining indistinct yet no longer separate from voice while behind him the radio continued, now indistinguishable as separate phrases, the cadence compressed into a continuous stream that filled the room without resolving into meaning as the wind pressed harder against the structure, the movement sustained, the intervals between gusts eliminated.

He spoke again, this time a longer phrase with its shape complete and intention unchanged, and the disturbance shifted again, not forming words but forming something, a structure within the irregularity that had not been present before, the pattern no longer entirely diffuse as the presence within the receiver began to hold itself in a way that suggested organization without clarity, and he remained where he was with the receiver held in place, the line extended between his hand and the wall, the connection still present in form but no longer in function, the space it was meant to cross remaining untraveled while the space within it had begun to fill with something that did not belong to either side and did not require the distance to be crossed in order to be heard.

The disturbance within the receiver did not resolve into clarity, but it did not remain diffuse, the pattern that had begun to form holding itself with greater consistency, the irregularity no longer shifting without direction but sustaining a structure that persisted across the space where silence had once been, the line not carrying his voice across distance yet no longer functioning as empty passage, the interior of it altered in a way that could not be separated from what he had sent into it.

He kept the receiver against his ear, his hand steady, the contact firm, his body aligned with the device as if movement might disrupt the condition that had begun to take shape within it, the cord extending from his hand to the base and into the wall, its path unchanged, its form intact, while what it held no longer corresponded to its purpose, and outside the house the wind continued to build, pressing against the structure without pause, the movement sustained, the intervals between gusts eliminated so that the house no longer returned to stillness, while behind him the radio voice remained continuous, its cadence compressed into an unbroken stream that filled the room without resolving into meaning.

He listened as the disturbance within the line held long enough to be tracked across time, not repeating but persisting, its presence no longer intermittent, the space within the receiver no longer neutral but occupied by something that remained even when he did not speak, the pattern not becoming clearer but becoming more defined, and he spoke again, the words measured, placed carefully, the phrase shaped with intention as the disturbance shifted immediately, not as reply and not as echo but as transformation, the pattern reorganizing at the moment his voice entered it, aligning with the rhythm of his speech without forming words, the presence within the line now responsive to what was introduced into it, not carrying his voice outward but altering itself in relation to it.

He remained still with the receiver pressed against his ear as the rest of the room receded completely in importance, the boundary of attention narrowing to the space within the line while the sound outside pressed harder against the house and the walls carried faint vibration that no longer remained subtle, the radio voice continuing without pause, its words indistinguishable as separate units, its cadence no longer allowing interpretation, and he spoke again, shorter this time, a single word placed clearly as the disturbance shifted again, more quickly and more precisely aligned with the moment of his voice, the pattern tightening, the structure holding more firmly, the presence within the receiver no longer diffuse but organized in a way that suggested proximity without location so that the line had not reached yet something within it had drawn nearer.

He adjusted the receiver slightly against his ear, increasing pressure without changing position, his hand tightening around it as if greater contact might bring clarity, the surface of the device unchanged, the cord still, the base unmoved, the connection appearing intact even as its function had been replaced, and the disturbance held before changing again not in response to his voice but on its own, the pattern shifting into a form that extended beyond the timing of his speech, the presence within the line no longer dependent on his input to sustain itself, the irregularity organizing into a sequence that carried duration without repetition, somethingwithin it maintaining itself across the absence of his words.

He did not speak and continued listening as the pattern remained, not resolving into language yet not remaining separate from it, the structure suggesting articulation without forming it, the movement within the linecarrying the shape of something that approached speech without becoming it, the boundary between what he sent and what returned no longer holding, while the sound outside continued to press against the house and the radio filled the room behind him with uninterrupted cadence, none of it intersecting with what was occurring within the receiver as the disturbance shifted again, not in distance but in form, the pattern beginning to align not only with the timing of speech but with its structure, the presence holding sequences that approached the shape of words without resolving into them.

He felt the change before he could have named it, the receiver no longer holding only sound but carrying something that pressed against the expectation of language, the boundary between signal and absence dissolving into a third condition that could not be placed within either, and he did not lower the receiver because the contact had become necessary, the line not reaching across the distance it was meant to cross yet what had entered it no longer requiring distance to be crossed, already present within the space that had once been empty and now beginning to take form.

The pattern within the receiver did not resolve into words, but it no longer remained separate from them, the structure that had formed holding itself in a way that suggested articulation without completing it, the disturbance no longer diffuse and no longer dependent on his voice, the presence within the line sustaining itself across time without requiring input, the space that had once carried sound across distance now occupied by something that did not need that distance to be crossed.

He kept the receiver against his ear, his hand steady, the contact firm, his body aligned with the device as if movement might interrupt what had begun to take form within it, the cord extending from his hand to the base and into the wall, its path unchanged, its form intact, while what it held no longer corresponded to its purpose, and outside the house the wind pressed against the structure without pause, the movement sustained, the intervals between gusts eliminated so that the house no longer returned to stillness, while behind him the radio voice continued in an unbroken stream, its cadence compressed, its words no longer distinguishable, the sound filling the room without resolving into meaning.

He listened as the pattern held, not repeating but persisting, its presence now continuous, the space within the receiver no longer neutral and no longer empty, the disturbance organized enough to suggest that it could become something more yet not resolving into clarity, and he did not speak because the change within the line no longer required his voice to sustain itself, the connection no longer dependent on transmission but on presence.

The pattern shifted again, not in response to anything he did but as part of its own continuation, the structure tightening, the sequences within it aligning more closely with the form of language, the intervals narrowing, the movement within the line approaching articulation without arriving at it, the presence within the receiver no longer indistinct but not yet defined, and he remained still with the receiver pressed against his ear as the rest of the room fell away in relevance, the boundary of attention fully contained within the space of the line while the sound outside continued to press against the house and the radio filled the room behind him with uninterrupted cadence, none of it intersecting with what was forming within the device.

The pattern changed, not gradually but in a single shift, the structure that had approached language crossing into it not fully but enough, a sound emerging that was not clear and not complete but shaped, a fragment of articulation that did not carry meaning yet did not remain separate from it, the presence within the line forming something that resembled speech without becoming it, the boundary between sound and word no longer holding as the fragment did not repeat yet did not disappear and the pattern continued, now altered and now capable of forming.

The next sound followed, closer to word, not yet one but nearer, the presence within the line no longer only responding and no longer only forming but beginning to produce, the structure sustaining itself while generating something that approached communication without crossing fully into it, and he remained where he was, listening without speaking as the pattern continued to shift, each sequence aligning more closely with the form of language, the intervals tightening, the structure holding, the presence within the receiver now occupying the space where voice had once passed through without resistance.

The line had not reached, but something had, not across the distance but into it, the boundary not crossed in the way it had been intended yet crossed in another direction, and he lowered the receiver not abruptly but with recognition, the contact no longer necessary to confirm what had occurred as the device remained in his hand, its form unchanged, its surface familiar, the cord still extending into the wall, the connection still present in appearance, and he did not return it to its base but held it at his side, the weight unchanged, the presence within it no longer dependent on proximity.

The room remained intact, the structure held, the radio continued, the wind pressed against the house, nothing within the visible space altered, but the line no longer functioned as a path between two points, it had become a place, and what had entered it did not require the distance to be crossed again because it had already arrived.

PART III

The Ones Who Lived Instead

STORY 8

The One Pulled First

BEFORE THE PULLING BEGAN, the rope existed as something that connected without strain, a line held between two points that did not require attention in order to remain secure, its tension balanced, its position stable, its purpose understood without being tested, running between hands that trusted it across a space that did not yet resist it, the fibers aligned, the length measured not in distance but in relation, each end held with the assumption that the other would remain where it was.

The rope had been placed deliberately, stretched across ground that held firm beneath it, the surface beneath both ends level enough that neither side required adjustment, the line itself resting slightly above the earth in a shallow curve that did not yet carry weight, requiring neither tightening nor checking, its presence sufficient to establish connection.

On one side, he stood with both hands around it, his grip secure but not forceful, the rope resting within his palms rather than pulled against them, his body aligned with the direction of the line without requiring correction, his stance steady, his footing firm, the space around him unchanged.

On the other side, the second position remained occupied though not fully visible from where he stood, the line extending outward beyond sight, disappearing past the edge of a slope where the ground fell away slightly before rising again, the distance not great and the connection not requiring sight to be trusted, the rope holding between them.

The air remained still at first, the space between them unaltered, the ground beneath the line stable, the surrounding area holding its shape without movement, there being no reason to pull and no reason to adjust, the connection existing in readiness rather than in use, until the first change came not through the rope but through the ground, a subtle shift beneath his feet that did not displace him but altered the way the surface held, the firmness remaining while the certainty of it changed, the alignment of weight no longer entirely fixed while the rope remained slack between his hands, its position unchanged.

He adjusted his grip slightly, not tightening it but re-centering it, his fingers shifting along the fibers to maintain contact as the ground beneath him settled into its altered hold, the rope not responding, the line remaining balanced, until the tension changed not from his end but from the other, a slight pull registering through the rope, not enough to draw him forward and not enough to require resistance, but enough to be felt as the fibers tightened within his hands and the curve of the line lifted slightly from where it had rested while the connection remained intact and he did not pull back because the change did not yet require it.

The tension eased and returned to neutral, the rope settling again between them, the moment not fully resolving before it came again with greater persistence, the pull stronger now, not sudden but sustained, the rope tightening further as the line lifted fully from the ground and drew straight between the two points, the slack removed so that the connection no longer rested but engaged, and he tightened his grip not in reaction but in recognition as the pull continued without variation, not erratic and not shifting but consistent, prompting him to lean back slightly, aligning his body against the direction of the force as his feet adjusted and his stance widened just enough to hold position while the rope held between his hands.

The other side did not release, the tension remaining and increasing not in bursts but in continuation, the line no longer marking connection alone but carrying force, and he did not step forward as the rope held and whatever had begun on the other side had not yet come into view but had already begun to pull.

The tension did not release after it first took hold, remaining in the rope as a condition rather than an event, the fibers drawn taut between his hands and the point beyond the slope where the other end disappeared from sight, the line no longer resting above the ground but carrying force cleanly from one side to the other, what had moments earlier existed in readiness now entering use without his choosing, the distinction between holding and resisting narrowing as the pull continued without interruption.

He did not pull back immediately with full force, at first only adjusting, his body responding in increments, his weight shifting rearward, his feet widening slightly to create a steadier base against the ground beneath him, the rope remaining straight, the fibers tightened to the point that their texture changed in his grip, no longer soft with slack but firm, the strands compacted under load in a way that made the line feel thinner and harder than before, the pull from the other end not jerking but drawing, and that difference mattered because a sudden motion could be met with reaction while this sustained pressure required sustained response, his muscles engaging not in a single act but in ongoing resistance.

He leaned back another fraction, the angle of his body shifting in relation to the line, his arms extending further, his elbows opening as the rope drew forward, his hands remaining fixed while the line itself moved within them in small increments, the fibers tightening and settling in ways that made clear the force from the other side had not only continued but increased, while the ground beneath his feet still held yet no longer with the same certainty, the surface bearing his weight but changing in how it supported him, his heels pressing harder, the soil compressing slightly, small stones shifting underfoot just enough to register that the ground itself was no longer passive but being drawn into the exchange.

He tightened his grip fully, his fingers closing until the rope pressed into his palms, the force carried through his hands into his wrists, forearms, and shoulders, the line no longer marking connection but becoming the path by which pressure moved, and he called out once toward the slope, his voice directed along the rope as if the line itself might carry sound more faithfully than the air, the word traveling outward but not returning in any identifiable way as the wind began to move across the ground more distinctly, not yet strong enough to disrupt balance but enough to interfere with the clarity of sound, leaving the rope as the more certain connection.

The pull strengthened, not sharply but enough that the difference between standing and being drawn forward became immediate, his front foot shifting slightly before he corrected it, the sole sliding and catching again as he drove his weight backward to recover, the adjustment succeeding but revealing how little stability remained, and he did not look away from the line though nothing new could be seen, the rope still disappearing over the slope, offering no visual indication of what lay beyond, yet through touch the information had become precise, the tension no longer merely greater but consistent, the draw maintaining direction so that whatever held the far end was no longer only under strain but moving.

He stepped back deliberately, placing his rear foot further behind him to widen his stance, then resetting the front foot carefully, attempting to create a stronger base from which to resist, the movement costing him distance that the rope took up immediately, the force from the other side not diminished but redistributed across his altered position, and he called out again, louder, not because he expected sound to succeed where tension already had, but because silence would concede that the line alone remained between them, his voice breaking across the open space and failing to return in any recognizable form.

The rope moved again within his hands, enough this time to burn, not sharply but unmistakably, the fibers dragging under load, advancing just enough that his grip had to tighten further to prevent losing ground, his fingers clamping down harder until the line held again, yet the movement had occurred, the force from the other side no longer theoretical but already gaining distance, and he lowered his center of gravity, bending through knees and hips, bringing his body closer to the line so that the pull passed through him more directly, the adjustment stabilizing him briefly as the rope steadied and the forward creep halted, the ground compressing further beneath his shoes.

Then the pull increased again, not visibly dramatic but absolute within the body, the line tightening to the point that all softness disappeared, the rope rigid, each fiber carrying the same command, his shoulders drawn forward, his arms nearing full extension, the muscles along his back and legs engaging completely, and for a brief moment he held position with everything aligned against the force before the imbalance declared itself, not through immediate loss of footing but through a change on the other side of the line, the angle shifting so that the pull no longer met him evenly, dipping and drawing forward so that the resistance he had established no longer matched it cleanly.

He felt the change at once, the pull no longer moving only through his arms and back but altering his balance from beneath, turning resistance into something that asked for movement, his front foot slipping again, further this time, the correction slower, harder, his body catching itself but only after the rope advanced another fraction through his hands before he locked it down again, the loss small but undeniable, and as he steadied himself and held the line, his breathing sharpening, his gaze fixed toward the slope where the rope disappeared, there remained nothing visible, only the taut line, the altered angle, and the certainty carried through his body that the other side had already shifted into motion first and that whatever had begun beyond sight was no longer waiting for him to respond but continuing to draw him toward it.

The line did not return to balance once the angle shifted, the change holding as a condition rather than resolving, the rope no longer running cleanly between two points but carrying a directional pull that altered how force moved through it, the tension uneven now, the draw from the other side no longer matching the resistance he could establish from where he stood, what had been held in opposition becoming misaligned, and that misalignment determining everything that followed.

He tightened his grip further, his hands closing until the rope pressed deeply into his palms, the fibers biting into the skin where earlier they had only rested, the contact no longer neutral but carrying consequence, the pressure transferring through his wrists and forearms into his shoulders, the entire length of his body engaged not in movement but in prevention, no longer attempting to pull the other side toward him because that possibility had already passed, the effort now only to remain where he was.

The rope advanced again, not in a single motion but in a sequence of small cumulative shifts, each one too slight on its own to be called movement yet together enough to draw him forward by degrees that could not be ignored, the fibers sliding within his grip, resisted and slowed but not entirely stopped, the burn in his hands increasing not sharply but continuously, friction marking where the line was no longer securely held but contested.

He shifted his footing again, stepping his rear foot further back in search of ground that might hold more firmly, but the surface behind him offered no greater stability, only a continuation of what had already begun, the soil compressing, small stones rolling under pressure, the edge of his footing no longer fixed but responding to the force that passed through him into the ground itself while the line did not slacken and the pull did not ease.

He lowered himself further, bending more deeply through his legs, bringing his center closer to the ground, directing his weight backward and downward in an attempt to counter the forward draw, the rope aligning more directly with his core, the force distributing more evenly across his body so that for a brief moment the movement slowed and the forward creep diminished and the line held where it was before resuming, not because he had lost position entirely but because the force from the other side had increased again with the same steady continuation that had defined it from the beginning, the rope tightening further, the fibers rigid enough that the line felt less like something held and more like something fixed that he had been attached to, the distinction between holding the rope and being held by it narrowing.

He drew in a breath, short and controlled, and adjusted his grip, sliding one hand slightly above the other to gain leverage, his fingers repositioning along the line to create a stronger hold, the movement costing him again as the rope advanced a fraction during the adjustment before he clamped down, the loss small but cumulative, the distance between him and the slope reduced by increments he had not chosen, and he called out again, louder, directing his voice along the line, the word shaped clearly and placed into it, but the sound did not return, the air carrying it outward and breaking it apart before it could resolve into anything that came back, leaving the rope as the only exchange between them, the only measure of what was happening beyond sight.

The angle shifted again, more pronounced this time, the line no longer pulling straight forward but downward and forward together, the slope beyond him no longer merely a drop in the ground but a change in level that now defined the direction of force, whatever held the far end having moved lower and in doing so altering the balance completely so that the pull no longer asked him to stand against it but to follow it downward, and he feltthe change in his legs first as the direction of strain shifted from backward resistance to downward instability, the ground beneath his front foot no longer sufficient to hold the altered angle, the pressure moving through him in a way that no longer aligned with his stance as his front foot slipped again, further than before, the correction slower and the recovery incomplete.

He caught himself but not fully, the rope advancing another measure as the burn in his hands sharpened and his grip tightened to its limit, the fibers pressing into skin that had begun to give under friction, the contact no longer sustainable without consequence while the line did not respond and the pull continued, and he stepped again, not backward but sideways, attempting to change the angle of resistance and find ground that might hold differently, his body turning slightly so the force might be redirected rather than met directly, the adjustment altering the strain without reducing it, the rope maintaining direction and the pull unchanged in its intent.

The ground beneath him shifted again, more noticeably now, the surface responding to the increased pressure, the edge of the slope closer than it had been moments before though he had not chosen to move toward it, the distance having been taken, and he glanced down briefly, just enough to register where he stood, the ground no longer level, the slope now within reach of his next step whether intended or not, returning his focus forward at once, the rope still central, the connection still the only measure.

The pull increased again not in speed but in inevitability, the line no longer advancing in increments that could be recovered, each shift now holding, each loss remaining, the ground beneath him no longer offering enough resistance to restore what had been taken, his front foot sliding again without immediate correction as his body tilted forward and he pulled back while the rope did not yield and the balance broke not completely but enough that when he caught himself again the recovery placed him closer to the slope than before, the distance reduced in a way that could not be reversed without slack that no longer existed in the line, the rope holding him in place though that place had changed.

He adjusted his stance once more though there was less ground to adjust into, his footing narrower, his balance more dependent on force than stability, the rope now carrying more of his weight than the ground beneath him as the pull continued unbroken and unanswered, and the certainty settled that the movement had not started with him, had not waited for him, and would not end because he resisted it, that the one on the other side had already been taken first and that what remained between them was not a connection to be held but a line along which that taking continued.

The loss of balance did not occur all at once, but it no longer remained something that could be corrected fully, each adjustment restoring less than what had been lost, each attempt to regain position revealing how much of it had already shifted beyond recovery, the rope continuing to carry force in a single direction while the ground beneath him ceased to function as a stable counterpoint to it. What had begun as resistance had become management of loss, and even that began to narrow.

He held the line with everything that remained available to him, his hands closed tight around it, the fibers cutting more deeply into his palms as the friction increased, the skin beginning to fail where pressure and movement met, the contact no longer something that could be maintained without cost, yet he did not release because release would not end the force, only remove his position within it. The rope no longer required him to pull in order to carry him. It only required him to remain connected.

His stance tightened, not by choice but by necessity, the space beneath his feet reducing with each small shift forward, the ground giving way in increments that could not be reversed, the edge of the slope no longer approaching but present, his footing narrowing as the angle of the pull drew him toward a place where standing would no longer function in the same way. He bent further, lowering himself instinctively as the direction of force pulled him downward as well as forward, the rope no longer horizontal, the line now defining a descent.

The pull did not accelerate.

It continued.

That continuity made it impossible to match, impossible to interrupt, the force not striking him in moments but carrying him between them, each second no longer distinct from the next, the movement passing through him without pause. He attempted to step back again, but the ground behind him no longer offered space enough to take the step fully, his foot finding less surface, the correction incomplete before the rope drew him forward again.

He tightened his grip again, though there was no additional strength left to apply, his hands closing until the rope pressed against bone, the fibers embedded into skin that had already begun to open, the sensation sharp now, no longer only pressure but damage, the contact no longer sustainable in the way it had been. The line did not respond to his effort. It did not slacken. It did not acknowledge resistance. It only continued to draw.

He shifted sideways once more, trying again to change the angle, to move away from the direct path of the pull, but the adjustment failed to alter the direction of force, the rope maintaining its line, the movement from the other side not deviating, not seeking him, but holding its course so that any change he made only repositioned him within the same direction. The slope beneath him no longer held a boundary he could stand above. It had become part of where he stood.

His front foot slipped again, not catching this time in the same way, the ground beneath it giving more fully, the surface no longer able to hold under the combination of his weight and the force moving through him, the motion downward now present within the forward draw. He pulled back hard, using what remained of his strength, his body straining against the line, the muscles in his arms and back tightening to their limit, but the rope did not yield, and the effort only slowed what continued.

He felt the shift before it completed, the moment where control ceased to be shared between him and the ground and transferred more fully into the line itself, his balance no longer anchored below him but suspended between his grip and the direction of pull. The distinction between standing and being held began to dissolve.

He called out once more, louder than before, the sound breaking from him with the force of exertion, his voice directed forward along the line, but the call did not return, the wind carrying it away and breaking it apart, the air no longer a medium through which connection could be confirmed. Only the rope remained.

The angle increased again.

Not by much.

But enough.

The line drew him downward more directly, the slope now fully engaged beneath him, his feet no longer finding level ground to resist against, the surface sliding beneath his soles, the small stones and loose soil shifting under the sustained pressure, his footing no longer fixed in any meaningful way. He tried to plant his feet again, to drive them into the ground, but the ground itself no longer held.

The rope advanced again.

Not suddenly.

But without pause.

The movement through his hands increased, the fibers sliding despite his grip, the burn in his palms intensifying as the line took more distance, his control over it diminishing not through a single failure but through the accumulation of what could not be held back. He tightened again, though the effort now produced less result, the rope continuing to move.

His body moved with it.

Not by choice.

By condition.

The pull did not need to overcome him.

It only needed to continue.

He stepped again, though it was no longer a step backward, but a placement downward along the slope, his foot finding unstable ground, his weight shifting forward despite his effort to hold it back, the motion no longer something he initiated but something he followed. The rope did not slacken.

He did not release.

The line held him in place.

But that place was no longer where he had been.

It was lower.

Closer to where the rope disappeared.

Closer to whatever had already been taken.

He tightened his grip once more, though the motion had begun to exceed what his hands could control, the fibers slipping again, the skin breaking further under the friction, the contact no longer stable, the hold no longer secure in the way it had been. The rope continued to move.

He moved with it.

The distinction between resisting and being drawn no longer held.

The slope took his weight.

The line took his position.

And what had begun on the other side no longer waited to be seen before it carried him toward it.

The movement did not break into a fall at once, but it no longer remained something he could govern, the slope beneath him no longer functioning as ground that could be held against, the surface giving under each attempt to plant his feet, the soil shifting, the small stones sliding, the angle drawing him forward so that every effort to stop became part of the motion itself, the rope remaining taut, the line no longer something he held but something that carried him, the distinction between resisting and following dissolving into a single condition that no longer required his agreement.

His hands remained locked around the rope, though the grip had changed from control to necessity, the fibers cutting deeply now into skin that had already broken, the friction no longer only heat but tearing, the contact no longer sustainable yet not releasable, the force moving through his hands into his body without interruption, the line not pausing, not easing, not offering any moment in which the motion could be reset, the pull not needing to increase because it only needed to continue.

He tried once more to plant his feet, driving them into the slope at an angle that might hold, his legs straining to anchor him against the downward draw, his body leaning back as far as it could without collapsing, but the ground beneath him did not provide resistance, only delay, the surface shifting again under pressure, the edge of his footing dissolving as quickly as it was established, the rope advancing through his hands in small unstoppable increments, the distance between him and where the line disappeared narrowing in a way that no longer allowed recovery.

He looked forward not because he could see what lay beyond but because the direction of the pull required it, the line leading him toward a point that remained out of sight, the slope steepening just enough that the descent became continuous rather than stepped, the motion no longer broken into moments of balance and correction but carrying him from one position to the next without pause while the rope held and the pull did not change, did not surge, did not falter, but remained, that constancy removing any remaining illusion that he could outlast it, that there might be a moment in which the force would lessen or shift or release enough for him to reclaim position, the line maintaining its direction, its tension, its demand without variation so that the movement through him was no longer negotiable.

His feet slipped again, both this time, the surface beneath them giving together so that the correction could not isolate one point of stability, his body dropping slightly, his knees bending further as he absorbed the change, but the lowering did not restore balance and only brought him closer to the line of descent, the rope pulling him forward again as soon as the motion settled, the distance taken not returned, and he tightened his grip once more though the strength required had already exceeded what remained available to him, his fingers closing as far as they could, the rope pressing against bone, the sensation no longer fully registering as pain but as pressure without boundary while the line continued to move despite his effort, the fibers sliding through his hands, resisted and slowed but not stopped so that the loss no longer remained incremental.

It had become continuous.

He took another step though it was no longer a step taken by choice, his foot placed where the slope allowed it, his weight following whether he intended it or not, the rope guiding the movement more than the ground beneath him, the direction no longer determined by his stance but by the line itself, and he did not release because the connection held but no longer held for him, holding him instead, the angle steepening further not dramatically but enough that standing no longer functioned as a stable position, his body tilting forward despite every effort to counter it, the rope drawing him into alignment with its direction, the resistance he applied only altering how quickly he moved, not whether he moved at all.

He called out again though the sound broke apart before it could return, the air no longer carrying anything back to him, the rope remaining the only exchange, the only measure, the only connection that persisted even as it no longer served the purpose for which it had been placed, whatever held the other end already having moved beyond the point where response could be given, and the rope moved faster now not abruptly but unmistakably, the friction in his hands intensifying, the fibers sliding with greater continuity, the skin no longer able to hold against it, the contact failing not in a single release but in the gradual loss of grip as the line advanced, the distance closing more quickly, the point where it disappeared no longer as far from him as it had been.

He tried once more to brace, to force his weight backward, to create a counterforce that might slow the movement enough to regain control, but the ground beneath him no longer responded, the slope carrying his weight forward, the rope carrying his position downward, the two no longer opposing each other but aligning in the same direction so that the effort did not fail suddenly but ceased to matter as the rope continued to pull and he continued to move, the distinction between those conditions no longer holding.

His hands tightened again though the strength required exceeded what remained, the fibers slipping further, the grip failing not through choice but through inevitability, the line continuing to move through him, the connection no longer something he could maintain as control but only as contact, and the slope dropped more sharply ahead as the line followed and he followed not because he chose to but because he had already been taken into its direction, the rope not breaking, not slackening, not releasing him, only continuing and in continuing carrying him past the point where standing had been possible, past the place where resistance had held, past the moment where he had still believed the connection could be controlled until what remained was only motion along the line that had begun on the other side.

The one on the other end had been pulled first, and he understood that now not as a possibility but as a condition already completed, the movement that had begun beyond sight having already taken hold before he had felt it, before he had tightened his grip, before he had attempted to resist, the line never having been equal between them once that first shift had occurred, and he did not let go not because holding would stop what followed but because the line was the only thing left that still connected him to where he had been, and as it carried him forward and down that connection remained even as everything else fell away, the rope the last point of contact between what had already been taken and what was now being taken after it.

STORY 9

The Empty Seat

Before the seat became something that marked absence, it existed as part of the arrangement that allowed the table to function as a place of shared presence, one position among others, its purpose defined not by who occupied it at any given moment but by the expectation that it would be filled. It stood in relation to the others, aligned with them, its distance from the table consistent, its angle unchanged, its presence unremarkable within the structure it helped complete.

The chair itself carried the quiet accumulation of use, the surface of its back worn slightly where hands had rested, the edges of its seat dulled by repetition, the legs marked faintly where they had been drawn across the floor and returned again, the wood holding the memory of movement without retaining any single moment as distinct. It did not stand apart from the others. It belonged within them.

Around the table, the remaining chairs held their positions, not evenly spaced but placed according to habit, each one oriented toward the center in a way that suggested attention rather than symmetry, the arrangement formed over time through use rather than design, the pattern held without needing to be corrected. The table itself carried what had most recently been placed upon it, objects arranged without finality, the surface neither cleared nor cluttered, the space prepared without being declared ready.

The room remained still, the air holding evenly, the sounds within it carrying without interruption, the faint hum of appliances from another space, the distant movement of air through vents, the structure of the house settling in ways that did not draw attention. The window along one wall admitted light that did not shift quickly, the outside visible but not yet pressing inward, the boundary between what was within the room and what lay beyond it still holding.

He moved within the space without immediate attention to the table, his actions directed toward small adjustments that did not alter the arrangement significantly, his hands placing and repositioning objects without fixing them, the motion of it habitual, unmarked, the room holding its shape as he moved through it. The chairs remained where they had been, each one maintaining its relation to the table.

The empty seat did not draw attention at first because it was not yet empty in a way that distinguished it from the others, its lack of occupation not yet meaningful, the expectation of presence not yet interrupted. It existed as part of the whole, not apart from it.

The first indication that it might not be filled did not come from the chair itself, but from the absence of movement around it, the lack of adjustment that would normally accompany arrival, the sound that did not occur, the shift in air that did not register, the space remaining undisturbed where it would have been changed. The room held.

The radio in another room carried faintly into this one, its voice steady, the cadence of information consistent, the words forming a sequence that could be followed without urgency, locations named, conditions described, instructions given in a tone that suggested continuity rather than interruption. The sound existed within the room but did not yet define it.

He turned slightly toward the table, his attention drawn not by what was present but by what had not occurred, the alignment of the chairs registering differently not because they had moved but because one of them had not been moved into use. The difference was small.

But it remained.

The light from the window continued to hold across the surface of the table, the shadows of the chairs falling in consistent lines, the space between them unchanged, yet the seat remained unoccupied in a way that no longer belonged to expectation alone, the absence beginning to register not as delay but as condition.

He stepped closer, not quickly, not slowly, the distance between himself and the table closing without interruption, his gaze settling on the empty chair, the position it held now distinct within the arrangement, the space it marked no longer neutral. The chair had not been moved.

Nothing in the room had shifted.

But something had not arrived.

And in not arriving, it had begun to define the space more clearly than anything that was present.

The chair did not change in its position, but it no longer remained interchangeable with the others, thespace it held beginning to carry weight that was not visible in its form, the absence no longer functioning as delay but as presence of a different kind, something that occupied the place without filling it, altering the way the arrangement could be read without altering the arrangement itself, the table remaining as it had been, the other chairs unchanged, yet the balance among them shifting in a way that could not be corrected by moving anything that was already there.

He stood near the edge of the table, his body oriented toward the empty seat, his attention fixed on it not because it demanded attention but because it no longer allowed itself to be ignored, the position it marked now distinct within the pattern, the space before it unbroken, the air above it undisturbed, the surface of the seat untouched so that nothing had been displaced yet something had not taken its place.

He reached toward the chair not to sit in it but to adjust it slightly, his hand resting against the back, the wood familiar beneath his palm, the contact confirming what had not changed in the object itself, the structure intact, the position stable, the legs evenly placed on the floor, and he shifted it a fraction of an inch, drawing it closer to the table as if the adjustment might restore alignment, the movement small enough that it did not disturb the arrangement of the others yet enough to mark intervention as the chair moved as expected and the correction held without resistance while the absence did not resolve.

He released it and stepped back, the distance between himself and the table reestablished, his gaze returning to the seat, the slight adjustment now part of the arrangement without altering what it signified, the space still unoccupied, the position still defined by what had not occurred, the room remaining unchanged as the radio voice continued from the other room with its cadence tightening slightly and the spacing between phrases reduced though the tone remained controlled, the message still forming a sequence that could be followed, the words entering the space without displacing anything within it so that the sound existed alongside the silence at the table without replacing or interrupting it.

He looked around the room briefly, not searching for anything in particular but confirming that nothing else had shifted, the objects in place, the surfaces unchanged, the light continuing to hold across the table, the window framing the outside without yet allowing it to press inward, the absence at the chair remaining the only alteration, and he moved closer again, aligning himself with the empty seat, standing where one would stand before taking it, his position mirroring the one that had not been filled, the perspective from which the table would be approached now occupied by him though he did not complete the motion of sitting but remained standing as the chair before him held its place unchanged.

His hand moved toward the seat itself, not resting on the back now but hovering above the surface where weight would normally settle, the distance between his palm and the wood held for a moment as if contact might confirm something beyond what could be seen, and he lowered his hand slowly until it touched the seat, the surface still, unmarked, unchanged, holding no impression of use, no warmth, no indication that it had carried weight recently so that he kept his hand there, the contact steady, as if duration might reveal what immediacy had not, the wood offering no response beyond what it had always offered, the material holding its form without memory of occupation while the absence remained intact.

He withdrew his hand and let it fall to his side, the gesture unmarked, the space before him unchanged, the chair remaining as it had been placed, its position now carrying a clarity that did not depend on explanation, the lack of occupation no longer temporary in the way it had first appeared as the room continued to hold, the radio voice shifting again with its cadence compressing further, the tone unchanged but urgency implied through repetition, the instructions overlapping slightly while still remaining external to the room as his attention stayed fixed on the chair, the absence now structured enough to be recognized as something that would not resolve through waiting alone, the expectation of arrival no longer sufficient to define the space and the possibility of it narrowing.

He pulled the chair out slightly, this time more than before, creating a space between it and the table that clearly marked it as available, the gesture deliberate and the movement larger, the intention clearer as the legs of the chair slid across the floor with a soft contained sound, the motion completing without resistance so that the chair stood open and the space before it unobstructed and defined, yet nothing followed, the gesture holding without response, the position remaining unfilled so that after a brief duration he pushed the chair back in, returning it to its place at the table, the movement reversing what he had done, the legs retracing their path across the floor, the alignment restored, the arrangement appearing again as it had before while the chair did not retain the gesture but only its position.

He stepped back once more, the distance between himself and the table increasing, the view of the arrangement widening, the empty seat now clearly one among others yet no longer equal to them, the absence it held no longer indistinguishable from delay but defined by what had not occurred and what no longer seemed likely to occur within the same frame of expectation, and the radio voice continued with its cadence now nearly continuous, the words no longer separated in the same way, the message advancing beyond the pace at which it could be absorbed fully while remaining external to the room, and within the space the table and chairs held their positions, the light remained steady, the air unchanged, and the empty seat remained where it had always been, its presence established not by occupation but by the absence that had begun to hold it in place.

The absence did not remain confined to the chair once it had been recognized, but began to extend into the arrangement around it, the space it marked altering not only its own position but the relation of everything connected to it, the other chairs no longer holding their places as equivalents but as positions defined in part by what was not present among them, the table itself carrying the absence across its surface so that what remained upon it appeared arranged around a place that had not been filled.

He remained standing near the edge of the table, his body oriented toward the empty seat, yet his attention began to shift across the arrangement, tracing the lines between positions, the distances between chairs, the way each angle now led back to the same point, the absence acting not as a gap but as a center around which the rest of the room had begun to organize. Nothing had moved.

But nothing remained neutral.

The objects on the table reflected the change in ways that did not require adjustment, their placement now appearing intentional in relation to the unoccupied space, the items closest to the empty seat taking on a proximity that suggested they belonged to it, while those further away seemed arranged in avoidance of it, though nothing had been placed with that intention. The absence had not been constructed.

It had been revealed.

He reached toward the table, his hand moving over the surface, not selecting anything in particular but passing through the arrangement as if testing whether the objects themselves would resist or confirm the shift that had begun, his fingers brushing lightly against one of the items nearest the empty seat, the contact slight, the object unmoved, yet the relation between it and the chair no longer felt incidental. He withdrew his hand.

The connection remained.

He moved to one side of the table, changing his position in relation to the chair, viewing the arrangement from a different angle, yet the absence did not diminish or relocate, it remained fixed in its position while continuing to shape how the rest of the room was perceived, the other chairs now appearing not only occupied or unoccupied but positioned in relation to the one that was not, their presence no longer complete on their own.

The radio voice continued from the other room, the cadence now nearly continuous, the words no longer separated clearly, the message advancing with a pressure that did not allow for pause, yet the sound remained external, unable to enter the space defined by the table in the same way, the absence holding a boundary that the voice did not cross.

He stepped back again, increasing the distance between himself and the table, the arrangement coming into fuller view, the pattern of chairs and objects and light now clearly structured around the empty seat, the absence no longer one element among others but the point through which the rest of the room could be understood. The light from the window fell across the table in the same direction as before, but the shadow cast by the empty chair appeared sharper, more defined, the space it occupied more clearly marked than the others.

He turned slightly, moving away from the table, his attention shifting outward into the rest of the room, testing whether the absence would remain confined to its original place or extend beyond it, and though the objects further away had not changed, they no longer held entirely independent positions, the awareness of the empty seat carrying with him so that even the surfaces beyond the table seemed arranged in relation to something not present within them.

He paused near the doorway, looking back toward the table, the distance between himself and the empty chair now greater, yet the absence did not lessen with distance, it held, maintaining its position while extending its influence outward, the room no longer divided into separate areas but connected through the single point that had not been filled.

The radio voice rose again, the instructions now urgent, the cadence compressed into an unbroken stream, yet he did not turn toward it, the message remaining outside the structure that had formed within the room, the absence at the table now the defining condition of the space.

He moved toward another chair, one of the occupied positions, and placed his hand on its back, the contact confirming its solidity, its presence intact, the surface warm from recent use, the difference between it and the empty seat now measurable through touch, the occupied position carrying evidence of weight, of presence, of completion, while the empty one carried none.

He released the chair and returned his attention to the empty seat, the distinction between them now clear not only in form but in condition, the absence no longer abstract but grounded in contrast, the difference between what had occurred and what had not.

He stepped closer once more, returning to the original position near the table, the arrangement unchanged, the chair still empty, yet the space it marked no longer capable of being read as temporary, the absence having extended itself through the room, through his movement, through his perception, until it had become the structure by which everything else was held.

Nothing had arrived.

Nothing had filled the seat.

And in remaining unfilled, it had begun to determine not only where things were, but what they meant.

The absence did not remain something he observed from a distance, but began to shape how he moved within the room, the choices he made no longer independent of the position it held, the path he took around the table adjusting in relation to the space that had not been filled, his body altering course without instruction as if the empty seat exerted a presence that did not require occupation in order to influence movement, what had first been recognized as difference becoming condition.

He circled the table slowly, not with purpose defined in advance but with attention fixed on how the arrangement held as he moved through it, each step shifting his angle of view while the absence remained fixed, the empty seat continuing to anchor the space regardless of where he stood, the other chairs appearing to rotate around it without actually moving, their positions constant yet their relation altered by his movement through them, the table itself not changing while the meaning of it did.

He paused at the far side, placing himself opposite the empty seat, the position one that would normally be occupied by another, the symmetry of it clear, the distance between chairs measured evenly across the surface, yet the balance did not hold, the presence of the other chairs not sufficient to counter what was missing, the empty seat carrying more weight than those that were filled, and he considered sitting not as a decision but as a possibility, the thought forming without completion, the motion beginning without being carried through, his body shifting slightly toward the chair opposite before stopping, the movement incomplete not because it could not be done but because it would not address what had already been established, since to sit would not fill the absence but only occupy space, and so he remained where he was without completing the action.

The radio voice continued from the other room, now fully continuous, the cadence compressed into a stream that no longer separated into distinct instructions, the urgency present but contained within its own structure, unable to enter the pattern that had formed at the table so that the sound persisted without intersecting, while he reached again toward the empty chair not to adjust it but to hold it in place, his hand resting against the back, the contact firm, the wood unmoving beneath his grip, the object unchanged in form yet the position it occupied carrying resistance not in the material but in the meaning it held, the chair not needing to move because it already marked what could not be altered.

He pulled it slightly again, not as before to open the space but to test whether the absence would shift with it, the legs sliding across the floor with a contained sound, the movement clear, the chair changing position in relation to the table, yet the absence did not follow the chair and remained where it had been, the space at the table continuing to hold what had not been filled even as the physical object moved away from it so that he stopped and held the chair in its altered position, the distinction becoming immediate as the chair was no longer the seat and the absence was.

He returned the chair to its place, aligning it again with the table, the legs settling into their previous position, the arrangement restored in form yet no longer the same in meaning, the seat now defined not by the object but by the space that persisted regardless of where the object was placed, and he withdrew his hand and stepped back, allowing the table to come fully into view again, the arrangement unchanged, the chairs positioned as before, the objects on the surface undisturbed, the light holding steady across it, yet the empty seat now entirely separate from the physical chair that marked it, the absence fixed in the space rather than in the object.

He moved away from the table again, increasing the distance between himself and the arrangement, testing whether separation would reduce the influence of what had formed, but the absence remained and extended beyond the immediate area, shaping how the room held together, the other surfaces now appearing arranged in relation to something not visible yet fully present, while the radio voice rose again with unmistakable urgency, the instructions overlapping in rapid succession, the message pressing forward without pause, yet he did not turn toward it because the sound remained external to the condition that had taken hold within the room, the absence at the table now the primary structure through which everything else was filtered.

He stopped near the doorway and looked back once more, the table centered in his view, the chairs surrounding it, the empty seat fixed among them, the arrangement complete in form but incomplete in function, the absence no longer awaiting resolution but holding itself as final, nothing having arrived, nothing having filled the space, and in not being filled the absence having separated itself from the object that had once defined it, becoming something that remained regardless of movement, regardless of adjustment, regardless of expectation so that the empty seat was no longer a place that could be taken but a condition that could only be recognized, and he did not move toward it again because the distance remained while the absence did not lessen with distance, holding instead and in holding defining the room more completely than anything within it.

The absence did not diminish with time and did not wait to be resolved, but continued to hold its position as something complete in itself, the space at the table no longer defined by expectation or delay but by the condition that had already taken shape, the empty seat not awaiting occupation but sustaining absence as its final form, the arrangement around it no longer temporary in its imbalance but stabilized by what had not occurred.

He remained near the doorway, his distance from the table established, yet the space between him and the empty seat did not reduce its clarity, the absence holding across that distance without weakening, the line of sight uninterrupted, the chair visible, the surface unchanged, the space before it still open, yet what it marked no longer dependent on proximity to be understood, the absence carrying through the room as a condition that did not require reinforcement.

The radio voice continued, now fully continuous, the cadence compressed beyond separation, the words overlapping into a single stream that no longer allowed for individual instruction to be distinguished, the urgency complete, the message no longer structured for reception, yet it remained external, unable to enter the pattern that had formed around the table, the absence holding a boundary that the sound did not cross, the room divided not by walls but by what had not been filled.

He took a step away from the doorway, not toward the table but along the edge of the room, his movement testing whether the absence would shift in relation to him, whether its position depended on where he stood, but the empty seat did not relocate and remained fixed while continuing to define the space from wherever it was observed, the room adjusting around it without moving, the absence remaining the center regardless of perspective.

He stopped and turned again toward the table, the arrangement unchanged, the chairs surrounding it, the objects resting where they had been, the light holding across the surface, yet the empty seat now entirely independent of the chair that marked it, the absence occupying the space regardless of the object, the condition persisting even if the chair were to be removed, the position no longer tied to form but to what had not occurred within it.

He moved back toward the table, not quickly and not slowly, the distance closing again without resistance, his attention returning fully to the empty seat, the space before it unchanged, the surface still unmarked, the absence still intact, and he reached toward it once more, his hand extending not to adjust or test but simply to enter the space that had been left unfilled so that his hand passed through the air above the seat without resistance and without response, the absence not reacting because it did not need to, already established as complete.

He lowered his hand and allowed it to rest against the edge of the table, the contact grounding him within the room, the surface solid, the structure intact, the arrangement unchanged in form yet entirely altered in meaning, the table no longer a place of shared presence but a surface organized around what had not been filled, and he remained there with his attention fixed on the empty seat, the absence no longer something that could be questioned or tested, the condition complete, the position fixed, the expectation of change no longer relevant.

The radio voice continued without interruption, the words indistinguishable, the cadence unbroken, the message no longer capable of being received in parts, yet it remained separate from the room, the absence at the table now the dominant structure through which everything else was understood, the sound existing but not entering, and he did not call out because there was nothing to call toward, the space that would have received the call remaining unfilled and therefore not allowing for response.

He stepped back once more, withdrawing from the table, the distance reestablished, the arrangement returning to full view, the chairs surrounding the table, the empty seat fixed among them, the absence now inseparable from the space it occupied, no longer distinct from the structure but part of it, nothing having arrived and nothing expected to arrive, the absence holding not as interruption but as completion, the empty seat no longer a place waiting to be taken but a place defined by what would not take it, the condition stabilized beyond reversal.

He turned away from the table and moved out of the room, the doorway passing around him as he stepped through, the space behind him remaining unchanged, the arrangement holding, the empty seat remaining where it had been, its absence fixed and its position complete, and he did not look back because nothing would alter if he did, the room continuing to hold, the table remaining, the chairs standing, and the empty seat, no longer waiting, defining the space by the absence it sustained, the place no longer one that could be filled but one that had already been determined by what would not arrive.

STORY 10

The List of Names

Before the list became something that could not be completed, it existed as a simple record, a sequence of names arranged in order, each one placed with the expectation that it would remain among others, the list itself defined not by any single entry but by the continuity of them, the sense that what began would extend, that each addition would follow the last without interruption. It lay on the surface where it had been set down, the page flat, the lines evenly spaced, the structure of it clear, the purpose contained within its form.

The paper carried the marks of use, the faint impressions left by earlier writing pressing lightly through from the sheet beneath it, the surface holding slight variations where pressure had been applied unevenly, the ink settling into the fibers with a consistency that suggested repetition rather than urgency. The names already written followed one another without deviation, each line complete, each entry contained within its space, the list not yet strained by what it held.

He stood over it, his body aligned with the surface, his attention directed downward, the pen resting between his fingers without yet touching the page, the position of his hand indicating readiness rather than action. The table beneath the paper remained steady, the objects around it undisturbed, the arrangement holding without requiring adjustment, the room itself carrying the quiet continuity of use.

The radio voice from another room entered faintly, the cadence steady, the words forming a sequence that did not yet demand attention, locations named, conditions described, instructions given in a tone that suggested ongoing movement without immediate urgency, the sound remaining part of the space without defining it.

He lowered the pen and wrote the next name, the motion controlled, the letters formed with the same care as those before, the line completed without hesitation, the ink settling into the page as it had with the others so that the addition did not alter the list but extended it, and he moved to the next line as the pen lifted briefly and returned, the spacing consistent, the structure maintained, the sequence continuing without interruption, the names remaining contained within their lines, each one separate and each one part of the whole.

Outside, the light held steady through the window, the air unchanged, the boundary between inside and outside still intact, the room maintaining its structure as he continued the task, the act of writing not yet influenced by anything beyond the page, and he wrote another name and then another, each one placed in its line, each one following the previous without deviation, the list extending downward across the page, the continuity of it intact and the expectation of completion unbroken.

The radio voice shifted slightly, the cadence tightening, the spacing between phrases reducing though the tone remained controlled, the message still forming a sequence that could be followed without interruption, and he did not turn toward it as the pen moved again and another name formed, the line completing, the ink settling, the sequence holding until he paused briefly not because the progression had broken but because the next line remained empty, the space waiting to be filled in the same way as those above it while the expectation of continuation still held and the structure of the list remained unchanged.

He lowered the pen again and began the next name, the first letter forming and then the second as the motion slowed without stopping, the line not completing immediately, the space remaining partially filled, the pen remaining in contact with the page while the name did not yet finish, the list holding even as the continuation itself began to change.

The line did not complete in the same way as those before it, the motion of his hand continuing yet no longer carrying the same certainty, the letters forming without interruption but not resolving into the same contained clarity, the shape of the name extending across the space as if the line itself resisted closure, the ink settling into the page while the sequence that had governed each entry no longer held with the same precision so that the list remained in place even as the act of adding to it had begun to change.

He kept the pen against the paper, finishing the name not with the same clean conclusion as the others but with a slight hesitation at the end of the final letter, the line extending a fraction further than intended before lifting, the ink marking the page in a way that did not match the entries above it, the difference small yet present, the structure of the list now carrying variation that could not be undone by adjustment.

He moved to the next line, the pen lifting and returning, the spacing maintained, the alignment unchanged, the expectation of continuation still guiding the movement of his hand, yet the pause before beginning was longer than before, the space holding for a moment as if the next entry required something not previously needed, the page remaining still beneath his hand as the act of writing itself no longer proceeded without interruption.

He began the next name, the first letter forming clearly and the second following and the third after it so that the sequence of motion remained intact, yet as the name extended the sense of completion that had accompanied each entry before did not arrive in the same way, the line continuing beyond the point where it should have resolved, the letters forming but not closing the space they occupied, the name stretching slightly within its line so that the ink marked the page without settling into the same contained boundary.

He lifted the pen, the name visible and recognizable in its form yet not fully held within the space of the line, the entry appearing complete while the sense of completion did not settle, and he looked at it briefly, his gaze tracing the letters as if to confirm what had been written, the shape intact yet the containment altered so that the space of the line held more than it should without revealing what had exceeded it.

He moved his attention upward along the list, the earlier names remaining as they had been, each one complete and contained within its line, the sequence stable, the structure intact, yet the difference between them and the most recent entries now visible not in the letters themselves but in how they occupied their space, the earlier names settled while the newer ones remained slightly extended, the boundary of each line no longer holding in the same way.

He returned to the next line, the pen hovering above the page as the space remained empty yet no longer held the same readiness, the radio voice continuing from the other room with its cadence tightening further and the spacing between phrases narrowing until the words began to overlap, the message pressing forward without pause, yet he did not turn toward it because the sound remained external to the page and unable to alter what had begun to shift within it.

He lowered the pen again and began another name, the letters forming with steady motion, yet as before the name did not resolve in the same way, the line extending slightly beyond its expected end, the ink marking the page without closing the space, the entry appearing complete while remaining unsettled so that the structure of the list now carried multiple points where completion did not fully hold.

He paused again, this time longer, his hand remaining above the page, the pen still in his grip, the next line empty, the space waiting as it had before yet no longer holding the same readiness, the expectation of continuation now accompanied by uncertainty so that repetition could no longer guarantee completion.

He looked again at the list as a whole, his gaze moving from the first name downward, tracing each entry in sequence, the earlier lines holding their form, the middle entries beginning to shift, the most recent ones no longer contained so that the list no longer remained uniform in how it held what had been written, the continuity of it altered without breaking entirely.

He returned to the next empty line and lowered the pen, beginning the first letter before stopping partway through its formation so that the ink marked only a portion of its shape, the line neither empty nor filled, the letter neither formed nor absent, and he held the pen there with its point still touching the page as the incomplete mark occupied the space, the line suspended between entry and absence without resolving into either.

He did not lift the pen and did not complete the letter, the motion halted without ending, the mark remaining partial, the space remaining open, the list still present yet no longer capable of proceeding in the same way, the act of naming now resisting completion not through interruption but through continuation that could no longer reach its end.

The incomplete letter did not resolve after he paused, and it did not remain isolated as a single interruption, but began to alter the way the rest of the list held together, the partial mark extending its influence across the entries above it so that the distinction between what had been completed and what had not began to weaken, the structure of the list no longer separating entries cleanly from one another but allowing uncertainty to move between them. What had first appeared as a single hesitation began to function as a condition.

He kept the pen against the page, the tip still resting where the letter had stopped, the ink no longer flowing in a continuous line yet not fully lifted from the surface, the contact sustained without completion, and as he held it there the partial letter seemed less like something unfinished and more like something that could not be finished, the shape of it resisting continuation not through obstruction but through the absence of a clear path forward.

He lifted the pen slightly, breaking contact with the page, the incomplete letter remaining where it had been formed, the mark stable, the ink settled, yet the sense of it unresolved, the space of the line still holding an opening that did not correspond to the pattern established above. He did not move immediately to correct it.

Instead, he looked at the entries above again, his gaze tracing the names in order, each one still legible, still recognizable, yet the clarity of their correspondence beginning to shift, the connection between the name and what it represented no longer holding with the same certainty, the letters remaining intact while the meaning they carried seemed less fixed, as if the list recorded forms that no longer pointed reliably beyond themselves.

He moved his attention from one name to the next, the sequence intact, the structure unchanged, yet the relation between entries no longer entirely stable, the names no longer simply following one another but beginning to exist alongside one another without clear separation, the boundaries of each line no longer fully containing what had been written there. The list had not been altered in its appearance.

But it no longer held in the same way.

He lowered the pen again, not to complete the unfinished letter but to begin another entry on the next line, his hand moving with the same practiced motion, the tip of the pen touching the page, the first letter forming, yet as it did the correspondence between the letters and the name they were meant to produce did not fully arrive, the sequence of strokes remaining correct while the sense of the name did not settle into recognition, the line forming without resolving into something that could be confirmed as belonging to anyone beyond the page.

He continued writing, the letters following one another in proper sequence, the shape of the name complete in form, yet as he finished it the result did not carry the same clarity as before, the entry existing on the page while not fully connecting to what it was meant to represent, the name present without being fully attached to its meaning.

He paused, the pen hovering above the completed line, his gaze moving across the entry, the letters legible, the structure intact, yet the recognition incomplete, the sense that the name should correspond to something beyond itself no longer assured. He moved his attention upward again, comparing it to the entries above, the earlier names still appearing stable yet now carrying the same slight uncertainty, as if the shift had moved backward through the list as well.

The radio voice continued from the other room, the cadence now compressed into a continuous stream, the words overlapping without separation, the message no longer structured in a way that allowed for individual parts to be received clearly, yet it remained external, unable to alter what had begun to change within the list itself.

He moved again to the next line, the pen lowering, the first letter forming, then the next, the motion steady, the sequence correct, yet the same displacement occurring, the letters assembling into a form that resembled a name without fully becoming one, the entry holding shape without holding correspondence, the list now carrying multiple lines that no longer pointed clearly beyond themselves.

He stopped again, his hand still, the pen resting lightly against the page, the accumulation of entries now forming a pattern that did not behave as it had before, the list no longer functioning as a record of identifiable names but as a surface of forms that resembled them without maintaining their connection, the act of writing no longer producing what it had been intended to produce.

He looked at the page as a whole, the lines extending downward, the earlier entries still recognizable, the newer ones less so, the incomplete letter still present where it had been left, the partial mark now part of a structure in which completion no longer held as a reliable outcome. The list remained.

But what it contained had begun to separate from what it meant.

He did not correct the incomplete letter.

He did not remove the names that no longer resolved.

He remained where he was, the pen in his hand, the page before him unchanged in form, yet altered in function, the act of naming no longer producing stable correspondence, the list continuing to extend while no longer holding what it extended for.

The list did not cease to function all at once, but it no longer held as a reliable structure, the entries remaining visible and ordered while their relation to what they were meant to record continued to loosen, the names retaining their form even as their correspondence thinned, the page carrying the appearance of continuity without sustaining it so that what had been written did not disappear yet no longer held in place.

He remained over the table, the pen still in his hand, the page before him unchanged in its physical arrangement, the lines evenly spaced, the entries aligned, the surface intact, yet the act of reading what had been written no longer returned the same clarity, the names no longer anchoring themselves to recognition in the way they had before as his gaze moved across them without settling into identification, each entry holding its form while failing to secure meaning.

He traced one entry with his eyes, following the letters from beginning to end, the shape complete, the structure intact, yet the sense of it did not arrive, the name failing to resolve into something that could be held beyond the page so that when he moved to the next entry the same condition held, the sequence continuing, each name retaining its form while losing its hold, the list no longer functioning as a stable record but as a series of shapes that resembled names without fully becoming them, the continuity now visual rather than meaningful.

He lowered the pen again not to continue the list in the same way but to test whether the act of writing could still produce what the earlier entries had held, his hand moving toward the next line, the tip of the pen touching the page, the first letter forming with care, the stroke deliberate, the motion controlled, yet as the second letter followed the same separation occurred, the form assembling correctly while the sense of the name did not take hold, the sequence of letters remaining unanchored so that when the entry completed it remained present on the page without attaching to anything beyond it.

He lifted the pen and paused with his hand hovering above the page, the next line empty yet no longer carrying the same invitation it had before, the expectation of continuation replaced by the awareness that continuation would not restore what had been lost, the act of writing no longer capable of reestablishing correspondence, while the radio voice from the other room continued as a fully compressed stream, the urgency unmistakable, the words overlapping beyond separation, yet remaining external and unable to enter the space of the page.

He moved his attention across the list again, no longer tracing individual names but taking in the page as a whole, the accumulation of entries forming a surface that appeared ordered while no longer holding the structure it represented, the lines extending downward, the earlier entries still recognizable in form, the later ones less so, the incomplete letter still present yet no longer distinct in its incompletion, the partial mark now indistinguishable in function from the completed entries around it.

He reached toward the page with his free hand, placing his fingers lightly against the paper near the center of the list, the contact grounding, the surface unchanged beneath his touch, the material holding its shape, the ink fixed in place, the physical structure intact even as its function had altered, and he pressed slightly as if pressure might restore what had shifted, yet the page did not respond and the entries did not recover their hold, the names remaining present without reattaching to what they were meant to signify.

He withdrew his hand and looked again at the entries, the repetition of forms now carrying a different weight, the accumulation no longer building toward completion but extending without resolution, the list continuing to grow while no longer serving the purpose for which it had been begun, and he lowered the penonce more andbegan another line, the letters forming as before, the motion steady, the sequence correct, the entry completing in shape while the same absence of correspondence remained so that the name existed on the page without securing identity.

He did not pause this time but moved immediately to the next line and wrote again, another sequence, another completed form, each one adding to the list without restoring its function, the accumulation increasing while the meaning continued to diminish, the page filling while the purpose of it emptied, the entries extending downward until the bottom margin approached, the space narrowing as the writing continued without resolving.

He stopped only when the line reached the edge of the page, the boundary imposed by the paper rather than the completion of the list, the entries now occupying the full surface, the structure intact in form yet no longer capable of holding what it had been meant to contain, and he held the pen above the final line without turning the page because continuation remained possible yet would not restore what had been lost, the list remaining in place while what it held no longer remained.

The list did not end when the page filled and did not complete in any way that corresponded to what it had been intended to hold, the final line reaching the margin without closing the sequence, the boundary of the paper marking a limit of space rather than a conclusion of the list, the entries remaining present while no longer securing what they named, the accumulation extending without resolution, the structure intact in form yet empty in function so that what had been written did not fail but no longer held.

He kept the pen in his hand above the bottom edge of the page, the final line complete in shape yet not in meaning, the names above it aligned, the spacing consistent, the surface filled, the page appearing finished while remaining incomplete, the sense of continuation not resolved by the absence of space but carried beyond it, the expectation of another line still present even though none remained on the sheet before him, and he did not turn the page at once because his hand remained still with the pen hovering as if the next entry might still be placed without requiring another surface, the space beyond the margin holding as possibility even while the physical structure of the page denied it, the list continuing not in form but in expectation, the sequence unbroken in intention even as it could no longer proceed in the same way.

The radio voice continued from the other room with its cadence fully compressed, the urgency complete, the words overlapping beyond separation so that the message was no longer structured for reception, yet it remained external, unable to enter the space of the page, the sound existing without altering what had already occurred within the list, the failure of correspondence contained entirely within the act of naming itself, and he lowered the pen slightly, bringing its tip close to the bottom margin without touching it as if the next name might begin at the edge where the surface ended, the motion slow and controlled, the expectation of continuation still guiding his hand even as the structure that had supported it no longer held, the line between what could be written and what could not now defined by the limit of the page rather than the completion of the list.

He stopped just before contact, the pen remaining above the paper without marking it, the continuation held as intention without becoming action, and he lifted the pen again, drawing it back slightly so that the motion withdrew without resolving, the position of his hand unchanged in relation to the page, the sequence extending without producing another entry, the absence of writing no longer signaling completion but the inability to complete, and he looked at the list as a whole, the page filled from top to bottom, the entries aligned, the earlier names still recognizable in form, the later ones less so, the incomplete letter still present among them yet no longer distinct in its incompletion from the instability of the entries around it, the entire surface carrying the same condition, the list no longer divided between what had been finished and what had not but unified in its inability to hold what it had been meant to contain.

He placed the pen down beside the page with the same controlled motion that had guided his writing, the object coming to rest on the table without altering the arrangement, the act of writing ending not through completion but through cessation, the tool no longer in use though the sequence it had produced remained unresolved, and he did not remove the page or cover it but left it where it was, the list visible, the entries present, the surface filled, the structure intact, the meaning absent, the names remaining on the page without securing what they named, the act of recording having produced form without preservation.

The radio voice continued without interruption, the urgency sustained, the words no longer separable, yet he did not turn toward it because the sound remained external, the condition of the list not influenced by what occurred beyond the room, the failure of correspondence complete within the space of the page, and he stepped back slightly from the table so that the distance between himself and the list increased, the page coming fully into view, the entire surface visible at once, the accumulation of entries now read as a single field rather than a sequence, the names no longer distinguishable in their function, the list no longer capable of being followed from beginning to end in a way that produced meaning beyond the page.

He turned away from the table and moved out of the room, his movement unmarked, the space holding its shape around him, the page remaining where it was, the list unchanged in form, the entries still aligned, the ink fixed, the structure intact, yet the purpose no longer present, the names no longer securing what they named, the act of naming no longer holding what it had begun to hold, and he did not look back because nothing within the list would change if he did, the page remaining, the names remaining, and the list, no longer capable of completion, continuing to hold only the forms of what had already been lost.

PART IV

The Ones Who Cannot Return

STORY 11

The House That Stands

BEFORE THE HOUSE BECAME something that could be measured by what it endured, it existed as a structure that held without needing to prove that it could, its walls upright, its foundation settled, its form complete in a way that did not require testing, standing where it had been placed, aligned with the ground beneath it, the weight distributed through its frame, the materials joined in ways that did not call attention to themselves so that the stability of it was assumed rather than observed.

The exterior carried the marks of time without displaying strain, the surfaces weathered in ways that suggested exposure without damage, the edges softened by seasons that had passed without altering the structure beneath them, the roof holding its line, the siding remaining fixed, the windows set within their frames without shift or distortion so that the house did not present itself as resistant but remained in place through continuity rather than demonstration.

Inside, the rooms held their arrangement, the walls defining space without movement, the floors level, the surfaces steady, the objects within them placed according to use rather than necessity, the air moving through the structure without interruption, the sounds within it carrying without distortion, the house functioning as it had been intended without requiring attention to maintain that function.

He moved through it without urgency, his path following familiar routes between rooms, his attention not fixed on any one point, the structure around him holding without requiring his awareness, the doors opening and closing as they had before, the floors supporting his steps without variation, the space responding to his presence without alteration so that his movement remained secondary to the stability that contained it.

The radio voice entered faintly from another room, the cadence steady, the words forming a sequence that did not yet demand attention, the message carrying information without pressing urgency, the sound present but not intrusive, the house containing it without allowing it to define the space.

Outside, the air remained still, the light steady across the exterior surfaces, the ground beneath the house holding firm, the structure aligned with it, the connection between what stood above and what supported it intact, the boundary between inside and outside clearly maintained so that nothing pressed inward and nothing shifted outward.

The first change did not announce itself as movement but as a shift in how the house held what was already in place, the structure remaining upright, the walls unchanged in position, yet the sense of alignment no longer entirely fixed, the relation between the house and the ground beneath it altering in a way that did not yet produce visible displacement but began to register as difference.

He stopped in the center of the room not because something had moved but because something had begun to register differently, the stillness no longer holding in the same way, the space around him carrying a slight variation that did not resolve into motion yet altered how the structure was perceived so that the house remained standing, the walls did not shift, the floor did not tilt, the structure held, and yet the condition of that holding had begun to change.

The change did not declare itself through visible movement, but it did not remain confined to perception alone, the structure continuing to hold in place while the manner of that holding began to alter, the alignment between elements no longer functioning as a single unified condition but as something that required continual adjustment to remain intact. The house did not shift.

But it no longer held without effort.

He remained where he had stopped, his position centered within the room, his attention no longer diffuse but directed toward the structure itself, not toward any single surface but toward the relation between them, the way the walls met the floor, the way the ceiling held above, the way the space between them carried a slight tension that had not been present before. Nothing had moved.

Yet nothing remained entirely settled.

The floor beneath his feet still lay level, the boards unbroken, the surface steady in appearance, yet the sense of support carried through it had changed, the contact between his weight and the structure no longer returning the same immediate certainty, the ground beneath the house no longer translating directly into stability above it, the connection holding while no longer remaining seamless.

He shifted his weight slightly, not enough to step, but enough to test the surface beneath him, the movement small, controlled, his foot pressing more firmly into the floor as if to confirm what had begun to feel uncertain, the boards responding as they always had, not bending, not giving way, yet the sensation of response arriving differently, as if the structure absorbed the pressure before returning it, the delay too slight to measure yet present enough to be felt.

The walls remained upright, their surfaces unmarked, the lines where they met the ceiling and floor unchanged, yet the sense of their position no longer fixed in the same way, the vertical alignment holding while requiring correction, the structure maintaining itself through continuous adjustment rather than through stillness. The house did not lean.

But it no longer stood without compensating.

The radio voice from the other room continued, the cadence tightening further, the words compressing into a more continuous stream, the message no longer spaced in a way that allowed each part to settle before the next arrived, yet the sound remained external, unable to enter the structure of what was occurring within the house itself, the shift contained entirely within the way the building held itself.

He moved a step toward the wall, not quickly, not with urgency, but with intention, his hand reaching out to make contact with the surface, the motion deliberate, the need for confirmation now present where none had been before, and when his palm met the wall the surface felt as it always had, solid, unmoving, the material unchanged, yet the contact carried a different quality, the resistance not immediate but absorbed and returned, the wall holding while no longer presenting itself as entirely fixed.

He kept his hand there for a moment, the pressure steady, his body aligned toward the surface, as if sustained contact might resolve what brief contact had not, yet the condition remained, the wall neither yielding nor fully returning the sense of solidity he expected, the structure holding without restoring certainty.

He withdrew his hand and stepped back, his gaze moving across the room, the arrangement unchanged, the objects in place, the surfaces steady in appearance, yet the relation between them now carrying the same subtle instability, the entire space holding itself together through a condition that no longer felt inherent.

The ceiling above remained level, the line where it met the walls straight, the structure intact, yet the sense of weight carried through it had shifted, the support it provided no longer translating directly into the space below, the load above held while requiring distribution that was no longer invisible, the house sustaining itself through balance rather than through fixed alignment.

He took another step, this time toward the center again, his movement cautious without being deliberate, his attention fixed not on where he moved but on how the structure responded, the floor still level beneath him, the walls still upright, the ceiling still above, yet the continuity between them now interrupted by something that could not be seen but could be felt, the house holding together through effort rather than through rest.

The radio voice rose again, the urgency now unmistakable, the cadence compressed into a continuous stream that no longer allowed separation between instructions, yet he did not turn toward it, the sound remaining outside the condition that had taken hold within the structure, the shift not coming from outside but from within the way the house maintained itself.

He stopped again, his position no longer centered by design but by necessity, the space around him holding without offering a stable reference point, the alignment between surfaces now dynamic rather than fixed, the house no longer a static structure but a system that continuously corrected itself to remain upright.

The walls did not crack.

The floor did not tilt.

The ceiling did not drop.

The house remained standing.

But it no longer stood in the same way.

The condition of its standing had changed from something given to something maintained, the structure no longer resting in stability but holding itself within it, the continuity of it dependent on constant adjustment that could not be seen yet could no longer be ignored.

And as he remained within it, the certainty that the house would continue to stand began to separate from the sense that it would continue to hold.

You're right—Part 3 still had step-fragment cadence ("The structure remained intact." / "But it no longer held as one." / short emphasis breaks) that interrupt the continuous strain you've built. This section needs to read as one sustained distribution of strain → loss of unity.

The house did not fail when the strain became perceptible, and it did not announce any single point at which its condition shifted from holding to something else, but the effort required to maintain that holding began to extend across the structure in ways that could no longer remain contained, the alignment between elements no longer correcting invisibly but distributing itself through the walls, the floor, and the ceiling so that each part maintained its position while no longer doing so independently, the structure remaining intact even as the unity of its holding began to separate.

He stood where he had stopped, his attention no longer moving across the room but fixed within it, the space around him now carrying a tension that did not resolve into motion yet did not remain at rest, the relation between surfaces no longer stable enough to disappear from awareness, the house presenting itself not as a fixed environment but as something actively sustaining its own form so that nothing had shifted and yet nothing remained passive.

The floor beneath him still lay level, the boards unbroken, the surface unchanged in appearance, yet the sense of support carried through it had altered further, the contact between his weight and the structure now requiring balance rather than providing it, his stance adjusting in small continuous ways that he did not initiate yet could not prevent, the alignment between his body and the house no longer immediate but negotiated so that he widened his footing slightly not in response to visible movement but in response to what the structure no longer supplied, the adjustment small yet necessary as the floor held him without offering stability as something given.

The walls remained upright, their surfaces unmarked, the lines where they met the ceiling and floor still straight, yet the sense of verticality no longer absolute, the structure maintaining its alignment through continuous correction, the surfaces appearing fixed while the condition that held them in place remained in motion beneath that appearance, and he moved his hand toward the wall again, slower this time, his palm coming to rest against the surface as before, the contact confirming solidity without restoring certainty as the wall absorbed the pressure of his touch before returning it, the delay more apparent now so that the structure no longer presented itself as immediate.

He pressed slightly and then released, the wall neither shifting nor resisting in a way that resolved the uncertainty, the surface unchanged while the condition of its holding remained altered, the structure maintaining itself through response rather than stillness, and he stepped back, his gaze lifting toward the ceiling, the plane above him still level, the lines clean, the structure intact, yet the weight it carried no longer translating directly into the space below, the support distributed through the house in a way that required constant balancing, the ceiling held not by fixed alignment but by the adjustment of what supported it.

The radio voice continued from the other room, now fully compressed, the urgency sustained, the words overlapping into a continuous stream, yet he did not turn toward it because the sound remained outside the condition that had taken hold within the house, the shift not driven by anything external but by the structure itself as he moved again, not toward any particular point but within the space, his steps measured not by intention but by the need to remain aligned within the changing condition, the floor still level beneath him yet no longer functioning as a fixed plane so that his movement adjusted to a structure that did not move and did not remain still.

The house held, the walls remained upright, the floor remained level, the ceiling remained above, yet the continuity between them no longer existed as something unified, the structure sustaining itself through distributed effort rather than inherent stability, each part holding its place while relying on the others in ways that no longer disappeared from awareness so that when he stopped again his position was no longer defined by the room but by the need to remain within it, the space around him no longer offering a stable reference point, the alignment between surfaces now something that had to be read rather than assumed.

The strain did not increase in force but increased in presence, what had been subtle becoming constant, the condition of adjustment no longer intermittent but continuous so that the structure no longer returned to stillness between corrections, the house holding itself in a state that no longer allowed rest, and the radio voice rose again with unmistakable urgency, the cadence unbroken, yet he remained where he was as the sound failed to intersect with what had already taken hold within the structure.

He stood within it, his body adjusting in ways he did not choose, his balance maintained not by the ground alone but by the relation between all that surrounded him, the house no longer supporting him as something stable but containing him within something that remained in the act of holding so that the structure did not fail and did continue, yet in continuing it no longer returned to what it had been and the certainty that it would remain standing no longer carried with it the certainty that it would remain the same.

The strain did not resolve into visible failure, but it no longer remained hidden within the structure, the effort required to maintain alignment now registering in ways that could be perceived without any single element giving way, the house continuing to stand while the condition of that standing began to appear, not as collapse but as exposure, the structure no longer concealing the work required to hold itself together so that what had once been invisible became part of what could be sensed.

He remained within the room, his position no longer stable in the way it had been, his body adjusting continuously in response to what the structure no longer provided, the floor still level beneath him yet no longer functioning as a fixed reference, the walls upright yet no longer absolute, the ceiling held above yet no longer distant from the effort that sustained it, the house no longer presenting itself as something that simply stood but as something that remained standing through ongoing correction.

He shifted again, a small movement, not chosen but required, his stance widening slightly as the balance he maintained depended less on the ground alone and more on the relation between all that surrounded him, the adjustment subtle yet constant, his body no longer resting within the structure but participating in its condition, the distinction between being supported and remaining upright beginning to blur.

The walls did not move outward or inward, but the sense of their position no longer held as fixed, the vertical lines appearing steady while requiring attention to remain so, the structure maintaining its form through continuous compensation, the surfaces holding their place while no longer doing so without effort, the house no longer resting in alignment but sustaining it.

He moved his hand toward the wall once more, not to confirm solidity but to measure the condition of holding itself, his palm pressing against the surface, the contact immediate yet altered, the resistance returning not as a direct response but as something mediated, the wall holding his pressure while distributing it through the structure, the sense of connection between his touch and the surface no longer singular but shared.

He removed his hand and looked upward again, the ceiling still level, the lines unbroken, yet the sense of weight now present within it, the support no longer silent, the load carried across the structure in ways that did not resolve into stillness, the house holding what it contained while revealing the effort required to do so.

The radio voice continued, now fully compressed into a continuous stream, the urgency unmistakable, the words overlapping into one another without separation, yet the sound remained external, unable to alter what had become visible within the house itself, the condition not imposed from outside but revealed from within the structure's own holding.

He took another step, not toward any destination but in response to the need to remain aligned within the space, his movement no longer guided by intention but by adjustment, the floor still level beneath him yet no longer sufficient to define position, his balance maintained through the relation between surfaces that no longer held independently.

The house did not crack.

The walls did not bow.

The ceiling did not descend.

The structure remained intact.

Yet the effort of its remaining had become visible, the condition of its standing no longer concealed within stillness but expressed through continuous adjustment, the house no longer defined by its stability but by its persistence.

He stopped again, his position held not by the structure alone but by his participation within it, the space around him no longer providing a stable reference but requiring constant reading, the alignment between elements now something that could be sensed rather than assumed, the house holding itself in a state that could not return to rest.

The strain did not increase beyond what could be held.

But it did not lessen.

It remained.

That persistence altered everything, the structure no longer moving toward failure but no longer capable of stillness, the house standing not as something stable but as something sustained, the condition of its holding now fully present.

The radio voice rose again, the urgency complete, the cadence unbroken, yet he did not turn toward it, the sound remaining outside the condition that had taken hold within the house, the structure now defining the space entirely.

He stood within it, his body adjusting continuously, his balance maintained through participation rather than support, the house no longer something that held him but something within which he remained held only as long as the structure continued to sustain itself.

And as he remained there, the distinction between a house that stands and a house that holds began to separate, the structure maintaining its form while no longer preserving the certainty that had once defined it.

The house did not fall when the strain became fully visible and did not reach a point at which its holding failed, but the condition of that holding no longer allowed for anything within it to remain unchanged, the structure continuing to stand while the certainty that had once defined it separated from the fact of its standing, the house no longer existing as something that could be relied upon in the way it had been even as it remained upright in form.

He stood within the room, his position maintained not by the stability of the structure but by continuous adjustment to it, the floor still level beneath him yet no longer sufficient to hold him without participation, the walls upright yet no longer absolute, the ceiling above yet no longer distant from the effort that sustained it, the house containing him without providing the condition that had once made that containment secure while the radio voice from the other room continued with its urgency fully compressed, the words overlapping beyond separation so that the message could no longer be followed, yet remaining external and unable to alter what had already taken hold within the structure itself.

He moved slightly, not toward any destination but in response to the need to remain aligned within the space, his body adjusting in ways that did not resolve into stillness, the house no longer offering rest but requiring participation, the relation between surfaces no longer something that could be ignored, the structure no longer passive but active in its holding as the walls remained in place with their lines unbroken and surfaces unchanged while the sense of their position no longer held as fixed, the vertical alignment sustained through continuous correction, the house maintaining its form not as a condition given but as something produced moment by moment without interruption.

He reached toward the wall once more, his hand making contact with the surface, the material unchanged, the solidity present, yet the response altered, the pressure of his touch absorbed and returned through the structure so that the sense of connection was no longer immediate but distributed, the wall holding without providing the certainty it once had, and he withdrew his hand and stepped back, his gaze moving across the room, the arrangement unchanged, the objects in place, the surfaces steady in appearance while the relation between them had fully altered, the house no longer functioning as a stable environment but as a system that maintained itself through ongoing effort.

The floor beneath him remained level, yet his stance did not settle, the need to adjust continuous, his balance maintained not through stillness but through response, the house no longer supporting him as something given but containing him within something sustained, and the ceiling above remained intact while the sense of weight carried through it persisted, the load distributed across the structure in ways that did not resolve into stillness, the house holding what it contained while revealing the effort required to do so as the radio voice continued unbroken and without entering the structure of what had taken hold within the house, the condition now complete.

He stopped moving not because the structure had returned to stillness but because his movement no longer altered his relation to it, the condition of holding constant, the house no longer capable of returning to what it had been even as it remained standing, nothing within it collapsing or breaking or giving way, yet the meaning of its standing no longer aligned with the certainty it had once carried, the structure defined not by its stability but by its persistence, the condition of its holding no longer silent but fully present within it.

He remained there for a moment longer, his body still adjusting, his balance maintained through participation rather than support, the house no longer something that held him but something within which he remained only as long as the structure continued to sustain itself, and then he turned and moved toward the doorway, his steps measured, his movement carried through the structure that continued to hold itself, the room remaining as it had been in form, the walls upright, the floor level, the ceiling intact, yet the condition of it no longer the same.

He stepped out of the house, the boundary passing around him as he crossed it, the air outside unchanged, the ground beneath him steady, the relation between his body and the surface immediate again, the stability returned not as something restored but as something separate from what he had left behind, and he did not turn back at once, his attention remaining forward while the house behind him continued to stand, its form unchanged, its structure intact, yet no longer holding in the way it had before, the persistence of it now distinct from the certainty it had once carried.

When he did look back, the house remained upright, the lines unbroken, the surfaces unchanged, nothing in its appearance marking what had altered within it, the structure continuing to stand as it had, the form preserved, yet the condition of that standing had separated from what it had once meant so that the house, though still there, no longer held what it had been built to hold.

STORY 12

The Road Back

Before the road became something that could no longer be followed in the way it had been intended, it existed as a clear line of return, a path that extended from where he stood toward a place that remained fixed in his understanding, the direction of it known, the distance measurable, the continuity between departure and arrival assumed without requiring confirmation so that it did not need to be interpreted but simply led back.

The surface of it carried the marks of use, the lines worn into it by repeated passage, the edges defined by what bordered it, the route holding its course without deviation, the structure of it sustained not by attention but by repetition so that the expectation that what had been traveled before could be traveled again remained intact and the road did not need to be read because it could be followed.

He stood at its beginning, his body oriented toward it, his position aligned with the direction it extended, the movement required of him not yet begun but already understood, the sequence of steps that would carry him forward assumed as something already held within him so that the act of returning did not require decision but recognition.

The radio voice entered faintly from behind him, the cadence steady, the words forming a sequence that did not yet demand attention, the message present but not intrusive, the sound carried without altering the space in which he stood, and he did not turn toward it because the road remained before him.

The first step did not alter the road and did not alter his relation to it, the surface holding beneath him as it had before, the direction unchanged, the path extending forward without interruption so that the act of moving along it confirmed what had already been known, that the way back remained open and the route intact.

Each step followed the last without variation, the surface consistent, the direction maintained, the alignment between where he was and where he intended to go holding without resistance so that the road did not require adjustment and his movement did not require correction as the distance shortened not in appearance but in expectation, the place toward which he moved remaining fixed and drawing the path forward through the continuity it sustained.

The radio voice shifted slightly, the cadence tightening and the spacing between phrases narrowing, yet the sound remained external and unable to alter what the road already provided, the direction continuing to hold without interference as he did not look away and the surface remained clear and the path extended forward so that for as long as he continued the certainty of return remained contained within the act of moving along it.

The road did not change in a way that could be seen at once, and it did not break or divide into separate paths, but the continuity that had defined it began to shift, the alignment between where he stood and where he believed he was going no longer holding with the same immediacy, the direction still present yet no longer entirely contained within the surface before him so that the act of following required something more than repetition.

He continued forward, his steps measured in the same way as before, the surface beneath him consistent, the path extending ahead without interruption, yet the sense of distance altered, not in length but in relation, the place toward which he moved no longer drawing the road toward it with the same certainty, the connection between movement and arrival beginning to loosen without fully breaking.

The edges of the road remained defined, the boundaries clear, the terrain on either side unchanged in appearance, yet the relation between the path and what surrounded it no longer entirely stable, the road holding its line while no longer fully determining the direction of travel, the space beyond it beginning to register in a way that did not align with the path itself.

He adjusted his stride slightly, not as a correction but as a response to what no longer held automatically, the motion small, the change in pace subtle, his body aligning with a condition that required attention where none had been needed before, the act of walking no longer sufficient in itself to sustain the certainty of return.

The radio voice continued behind him, the cadence tightening further and the words compressing into a more continuous stream, yet the sound remained external and unable to define the direction in which he moved, the message present but not intersecting with the path beneath his feet, so that he did not turn and the road remained before him even as the sense of forward no longer carried the same meaning it had at the beginning.

He moved again, step following step, the surface consistent and the line of the road unbroken, yet the relation between his movement and the direction it was meant to produce began to shift, the path no longer translating directly into return, the distance no longer reducing in the same way, and the expectation of arrival no longer contained within the act of continuing.

The horizon held where it had been, the line of sight unchanged and the path extending toward it without deviation, yet the point toward which he moved no longer appeared to draw closer in the same way, the road maintaining its form while altering its function, the sequence of movement no longer guaranteeing the outcome it once had.

He slowed slightly, not stopping but reducing the pace of his steps, the change arising from within the act of moving itself, his body responding to a condition that no longer aligned with expectation, the road still beneath him yet no longer sufficient to determine where it led or what it would produce if followed to its end.

The edges of the path began to feel less fixed, not shifting in position but in relation, the boundary between the road and the ground beside it no longer holding as a clear division, the distinction between where he walked and where he did not walk becoming less certain, the surface remaining visible while the meaning of that surface began to change.

He stepped again, placing his foot where the road appeared to be, the contact firm and the ground supporting him as before, yet the sense of being on the path no longer fully contained within that contact, the alignment between position and direction no longer assured by placement alone, so that the act of continuing required something beyond simply remaining on the road.

The radio voice rose again behind him, urgency more apparent and the cadence compressed into a continuous stream, yet he did not turn and the sound remained behind him while the road remained before him, the relation between them unchanged even as the relation between him and the road continued to shift.

He continued forward, not because the path held him within its direction but because stopping would not restore what had already begun to change, the movement sustained not by certainty but by continuation, the road still extending ahead while no longer carrying the full weight of return.

The surface remained intact, the path did not divide, and the direction did not disappear, yet the continuity between them no longer held as something complete, the act of following no longer equivalent to arriving, and the road extended forward while no longer fully leading back.

You're right—Part 3 still had residual fragmentation and rhythmic breaks ("He did not turn." / "He walked." / short declarative closures) that interrupt the paragraph standard and reduce density.

The change did not arrive as a break in the road, nor as a visible interruption that would have allowed him to stop and name it, but as a gradual failure in the way the path held its relation to what lay beyond it, the surface remaining intact while the continuity it had once carried began to separate from the outcome it had once produced, so that the road still extended forward and his body still moved along it, yet the correspondence between direction and destination no longer held as a single structure and the path continued to offer itself while no longer ensuring what it once led toward.

He continued walking, not because the certainty remained, but because the absence of certainty did not yet produce an alternative, the act of stopping offering no correction to what had already shifted, and the road beneath him still providing the only visible line of movement, the surface not failing under his weight and the ground not giving way, yet the sense of being carried forward toward a fixed point no longer aligning with what he felt as he moved, the distance no longer shortening in the way that had once defined progress.

The horizon remained visible, butits relation to the road altered, no longer serving as a point toward which the path resolved, but as something that remained at a distance regardless of the steps taken, the line of sight holding steady while the meaning of that line detached from movement, the road not curving to correct itself and not dividing to offer options, but persisting in a straight extension that no longer confirmed its purpose.

He adjusted his pace again, this time more noticeably, the rhythm of his steps no longer automatic but measured, his body attempting to align with a condition that could not be corrected through variation in movement, the effort to remain on the road no longer producing the same result as before, and the act of continuing beginning to feel less like following and more like maintaining position within a structure that no longer led anywhere beyond itself.

The radio voice behind him intensified, the cadence no longer merely compressed but insistent, the language sharpening into directives that named locations, routes, and conditions that required response, yet the words did not attach to the road before him and the information failed to intersect with the path he occupied, so that turning toward it would not alter the fact that the road remained where it was and continued to extend forward without changing its form, and the decision not to turn arose not from resistance but from recognition that the voice could not restore what the road had lost.

He continued forward, though the act of continuing no longer carried the same meaning, the distance beneath his feet accumulating without translating into approach, the place he had intended to reach no longer drawing nearer in response to movement, the path remaining consistent while the outcome it once guaranteed had separated from it, leaving only the structure of the road without the certainty of where it led.

The edges of the path grew less reliable, not dissolving but failing to define the boundary with the same authority, the ground beside it appearing no different from the surface beneath his feet, the distinction between path and surrounding terrain becoming less decisive, so that remaining on the road required attention that had not been necessary before, each step placed with greater care not because the surface had become unstable but because its meaning had.

The air around him carried a pressure that had not been present earlier, not the force of wind as in a storm, but a density that seemed to hold movement in place, the space through which he walked no longer neutral but resistant in a way that did not impede his steps yet altered the sense of passing through it, the road extending within this altered condition unchanged in form but affected in function, the act of moving forward no longer producing the same relation to distance.

He slowed again, though he did not stop, the reduction in pace arising from the recognition that speed would not restore alignment and that the road would not correct itself through greater effort, the condition in which he moved not responding to adjustment in the way ordinary paths did, the steps continuing while the outcome did not follow, the structure of movement remaining intact even as its purpose no longer held.

The horizon remained where it had been and the road still pointed toward it, yet the connection between them no longer held as a promise, the line of the path no longer guaranteeing arrival, the distance between where he stood and where he intended to go no longer measurable in the way it had once been, the road extending but not resolving, the direction holding while its meaning failed.

He continued because the act of continuing remained the only structure available to him, the movement sustained without confirmation, the path followed without assurance, the road carrying him forward without bringing him closer, while behind him the radio voice reached a point where it could no longer be dismissed as background, the urgency fully present and the language no longer informational but directive, yet still unable to replace the path beneath his feet, leaving him within a condition where the only visible way forward no longer produced return, and where each step confirmed what the last had already suggested, that the road no longer led back in the way it had been meant to and that continuing along it would not restore what had been lost when the alignment between movement and arrival first began to fail.

You're right again—Part 4 still had residual fragmentation (short standalone lines like "He stopped." / "The road remained before him." / "Nothing reoriented.") that break the paragraph standard and thin the density at exactly the moment the narrative should feel most structurally heavy.

The failure did not arrive as collapse, and it did not present itself as a moment that could be marked and separated from what had come before, but as the point at which the road no longer functioned as a path even while remaining visibly intact, the surface continuing beneath his feet while the relation between movement and direction ceased to produce anything beyond itself, so that the act of walking no longer carried him toward a place but held him within a structure that extended without resolving.

He continued forward because stopping did not offer correction and because the road still existed in front of him, yet the continuation had begun to change in quality, no longer sustained by expectation but by the absence of alternatives, the steps following one another in sequence without producing progress, the distance beneath him accumulating without altering his relation to where he had begun or where he believed he was going.

The horizon no longer functioned as a point of orientation, remaining fixed at the same distance regardless of movement, its presence no longer connected to the road that extended toward it, the line of sight detached from the structure of the path so that the direction indicated by one did not correspond to the outcome suggested by the other, and although the road remained straight, the surface continuous, and the edges visible, none of these features produced guidance in the way they had before, leaving the act of following indistinguishable from remaining in place.

He slowed further, not as a deliberate decision but as a consequence of the diminishing relation between effort and result, his body responding to a condition in which increased movement did not alter outcome, the pace reducing until each step required confirmation before the next could occur, not because the ground was unstable but because its function had altered and the road no longer carried him but simply received him.

The radio voice behind him had become fully directive, the cadence compressed into urgency and the language naming routes, instructions, and alternatives, yet none of what it offered aligned with the road beneath his feet, the information unable to attach to the condition in which he stood, so that turning toward it would not restore direction but only introduce another structure that could not intersect with the one he occupied, leaving him facing forward not because it was correct but because nothing else could be made to hold.

The edges of the road ceased to function as boundaries, not disappearing but losing their authority, the ground beside the path no longer distinguishable in purpose from the surface beneath him, so that stepping off would not produce a different outcome and remaining on would not restore the one that had been lost, the distinction between path and non-path dissolving not in form but in function and leaving only surface without direction.

He stepped again, placing his foot where the road remained visible, the contact firm and unchanged, yet the act of placing it no longer contributed to movement in any meaningful sense, the sequence continuing while the effect failed, the structure of walking persisting without the result it once produced.

The air around him thickened further, not resisting his body but holding it within a condition where movement did not translate into passage, the space through which he walked no longer opening as he moved through it but remaining constant, as if the distance between one point and another could no longer be reduced through motion, and the road extended within this condition unchanged in appearance yet altered in its capacity to function as a means of travel.

He came to stillness within the path, and the absence of movement did not restore what had been lost, the road remaining before him unchanged while the horizon held its position and the distance did not resolve, so that standing and walking no longer produced different relations to the space and the condition remained constant regardless of action.

He turned slightly, not fully reversing direction but altering his alignment enough to test whether orientation alone might restore what movement had lost, and then he stepped again into a position that did not correspond to the path's original direction, yet the surface held without producing change, the outcome remaining fixed, the road unresponsive to variation in position or intent.

He turned further, and the path remained, the horizon remained, and nothing within the structure reoriented to meet him, so that the act of turning failed in the same way as the act of continuing, each movement absorbed without effect.

He resumed walking, not because direction had been restored but because remaining still did not produce clarity, the movement continuing as an action without outcome, the road receiving each step without translating it into progress, and the recognition forming not as a sudden realization but as a condition that replaced expectation, that the road could no longer be used in the way it had been intended, that following it would not return him to where he had begun, and that the structure that had once carried meaning no longer did so even while remaining visible and intact.

He continued because stopping did not alter that fact, because turning did not alter it either, and because the road remained even as it no longer led, leaving him within a structure that still extended forward while no longer bringing him closer.

The road remained where it had always been, extending forward with the same visible continuity that had first invited movement, the surface unbroken, the line of it clear against the surrounding ground, and the direction still present even after the function that had once defined it had fallen away, so that nothing within its appearance suggested that it could no longer be used while everything within his experience confirmed that it could not be followed in the way it had been intended.

He stood within it without attempting to resolve the condition, his body aligned with the path yet no longer oriented by it, the relation between position and purpose having separated in a way that did not require explanation because it could be felt in every step that no longer produced what it once had, and the road did not change in response to his stillness or correct itself when he shifted his weight, the structure remaining consistent while the meaning that had once moved through it no longer returned.

The radio voice had not ceased, but it no longer entered as something that could alter the condition, the urgency fully formed and the language continuing to name what should be done, where to go, and how to proceed, yet the instructions did not attach to the space in which he stood, the direction they offered unable to intersect with the path that remained beneath his feet, so that the presence of guidance did not restore the capacity to follow.

He stepped again, not because the act would produce return, but because the absence of action would not change the condition, the movement no longer guided by expectation but sustained as something that could still be done even when it no longer carried him toward a place, the surface receiving his weight as it always had, the ground holding firm, and the alignment of his body with the road preserved even as the relation between movement and destination remained absent.

The horizon held its position without drawing nearer, the distance unchanged regardless of the steps taken, the line of sight remaining constant while the meaning of that line no longer corresponded to arrival, so that the act of looking forward no longer implied that anything would be reached, and the road pointed toward it in the same way, the direction unchanged even as the connection between direction and outcome remained severed.

He continued walking, not as a correction and not as an attempt to restore what had been lost, but as the continuation of a motion that still existed even after its purpose had failed, the steps following one another in sequence without producing change, the distance beneath him accumulating without altering his relation to the place he had intended to reach, the road extending and his movement continuing within it even as the absence of return did not interrupt the act of continuing.

The edges of the path remained visible without defining anything, the ground beside it no longer functioning as something different, the distinction between being on the road and being off it no longer producing consequence, so that the choice to remain within its boundaries did not carry meaning in the way it once had, the structure persisting even after its authority had ended.

At times he slowed, and at times his pace increased slightly, not because either would change the outcome, but because the body continued to adjust even when adjustment no longer produced result, the rhythm of movement continuing within a condition that did not respond to it, the steps not failing and the ground not resisting, yet the act of walking remaining separate from the act of arriving.

The radio voice continued behind him, still urgent, still precise, still naming directions that could not be taken from where he stood, and he did not turn because turning would not create a path that intersected with the one he occupied, leaving him within a condition where information remained present without becoming usable and where the presence of instruction did not restore the capacity to follow.

He did not leave the road, not because it still led, but because leaving it would not restore direction, and he continued within it, the movement sustained not by belief but by the absence of an alternative that could be made to hold, the structure of the path still available even as its function had been lost, the act of walking continuing without producing what it once had.

There were moments when his steps slowed to the point where they nearly ceased, his body approaching stillness without fully entering it, and in those moments the condition did not change, the road remaining as it was, the horizon holding its place, and the distance refusing to resolve, so that even the edge of stopping did not offer a different relation to what remained.

He resumed, not because resuming altered anything, but because the motion had not ended, the continuation existing even when the purpose had not, the path extending forward without leading and the body moving within it without arriving, the structure holding without resolving so that the road remained and he remained within it and the act of continuing did not bring him back.

STORY 13

The Field That Changed

Before the field became something that could no longer be read in the way it had always been read, it existed as an open surface whose meaning was held in its continuity, the ground extending outward without obstruction, the boundaries visible from any point within it, and the relation between position and direction remaining stable enough that a person standing anywhere within its span could orient themselves without effort, understanding where they were and where they could go without needing to test it.

The field had been used in ways that reinforced that clarity, its surface marked by repeated passage, the faint lines of movement crossing it in patterns that did not need to be followed precisely in order to be useful, the paths overlapping without confusion because they all led toward places that remained fixed, the edges of the field corresponding to what lay beyond them, the road along one side, the tree line along another, and the low rise toward the far boundary that signaled where the ground would begin to change.

He entered the field from the same point he had always used, the opening between two posts that no longer held a gate but still marked transition, his body passing from the contained structure of the yard into the open span beyond it, the shift not requiring acknowledgment because it had been made so many times before that it no longer carried distinction, and the ground beneath his feet felt as it always had, firm enough to hold and uneven enough to register the natural variation of the land, the grass worn slightly where others had crossed and thicker where it had not been disturbed.

The sky above remained consistent with what the morning had suggested, the light spreading evenly without interruption, the clouds present but not forming into anything that required interpretation, and the air carrying no pressure that would indicate change, so that the field held its shape beneath that sky, the openness of it unchanged, the distance across it measurable by sight and by memory, and the far edge remaining where it had always been.

He began walking without hesitation, his steps aligning with the direction he intended to follow, the line of movement clear enough that it did not require adjustment, the field offering itself as a surface that could be crossed without resistance, and the paths that had formed through use were still visible, though faint, yet he did not need to choose one because the act of crossing did not depend on staying within them, the ground itself sufficient to support the direction he carried.

As he moved further into the field, the relation between where he stood and where he was going remained intact, the distance closing in the expected way, the far edge appearing gradually nearer without altering its position, the ground rising slightly where it always had, and the familiar change in elevation confirming that he was moving along the same line he had followed before, so that nothing within the field required reconsideration and nothing suggested that it would behave differently than it had in every previous crossing.

The wind moved lightly across the surface, not in a way that disrupted balance but in a pattern that carried across the grass, bending it in small, consistent waves that moved from one edge of the field toward the other, the motion visible but not forceful, the air remaining within the range of what could beignored, and the sound of it did not rise above the level of background as the field absorbed it without altering its own stillness.

He continued at the same pace, the rhythm of his steps unbroken and the direction held without correction, his position within the field corresponding to the path he intended to take, while the boundaries remained visible from where he was, the tree line steady, the road unchanged, and the rise ahead aligning with the memory he carried of how the field extended and where it ended, so that the ground beneath him confirmed what he already knew, each step reinforcing the stability of the surface and the reliability of the space.

There was no reason to stop and no reason to adjust, the field providing everything required for movement, the openness of it allowing for direction without constraint, and the continuity of it holding without interruption, so that the act of crossing remained what it had always been, a passage from one side to the other that did not require interpretation, only continuation.

He moved further into it, the distance behind him increasing in the same way the distance ahead decreased, the relation between the two remaining consistent, the midpoint of the field approaching without needing to be marked, the sense of being within the center of it arising naturally as the edges receded equally in all directions, and the field held him within that balance, the openness extending outward in every direction while still allowing him to know where he was, so that nothing shifted and nothing misaligned as the field remained what it had always been while he continued across it.

The change did not announce itself as a visible alteration in the field, and nothing within the surface suggested that the structure which had held so consistently was no longer fully intact, yet the relation between where he stood and where he intended to go began to shift in a way that did not present itself as error but as a slight misalignment that could not be located within the ground or within his movement. The openness remained, the boundaries still visible, and the rise ahead still aligned with memory, yet something within the field no longer confirmed direction in the same way, the act of moving forward continuing without producing the same correspondence between intention and position.

He continued walking at the same pace, the rhythm of his steps unchanged, the ground beneath him steady and responsive, yet the distance ahead did not reduce in the same way as before, the far edge appearing neither closer nor farther, but held in a position that no longer responded to movement with the clarity it once had. The field did not expand, and it did not contract, yet the measure of crossing it no longer behaved in a way that could be confirmed through sight or through memory, the relation between effort and outcome beginning to loosen without breaking.

The paths that had once crossed the field in faint but reliable lines became less distinct, not erased but less meaningful, their direction no longer clearly corresponding to the boundaries they had once connected, so that following them would not guarantee alignment with the edges of the field in the way it had before. He did not adjust toward them, but their presence no longer reinforced his own line of movement, and the surface beneath him no longer carried the same quiet assurance that direction had already been established.

The wind moved across the field again, but the pattern altered slightly, no longer traveling in a consistent direction from one boundary to another, but shifting in intervals that did not align with the visible space, the grass bending in one direction and then another without a clear origin, the motion remaining gentle yet no longer uniform. The change was not strong enough to disrupt balance, but it introduced variation where there had been consistency, and the field absorbed that variation without correcting it.

He adjusted his stride without intending to, a slight alteration in pace that arose from the condition itself rather than from decision, his body responding to something that did not resolve into a visible cause, the rhythm of his movement no longer entirely self-sustaining. The act of walking required a degree of attention that had not been present before, not because the ground had become unstable, but because the meaning of the ground had begun to shift.

The boundaries of the field remained visible, but their relation to his position no longer held with the same precision, the tree line appearing consistent yet not fully anchoring his direction, the road along the edge still present yet no longer clearly defining orientation. The rise ahead remained, but it did not draw closer in the same way, and the relation between that elevation and his movement toward it began to lose its clarity, as though the field no longer translated distance in a way that could be confirmed through movement.

He continued forward because stopping did not offer resolution, the field still providing the only surface available for movement, yet the continuation no longer carried the same assurance, the openness of the space no longer guaranteeing alignment between intention and outcome. The distance behind him did not feel as though it had increased proportionally to the steps he had taken, and the midpoint he had passed through no longer held in memory as a fixed position within the field.

The air remained consistent in temperature and weight, yet the sense of moving through it altered slightly, the space no longer entirely neutral, as though the field extended not only across the ground but through the air itself, holding him within a condition that did not resist movement yet did not fully permit it to produce change. The difference was slight, not enough to interrupt the act of walking, but present enough that the continuity of crossing could no longer be assumed.

He looked toward the far edge again, not searching for change but confirming position, yet the confirmation did not complete itself, the boundary remaining visible while failing to anchor his movement in the way it had before. The field did not deny him direction, but it no longer provided it.

He continued walking, the steps following one another in the same measured sequence, the ground holding firm beneath him, the surface unchanged, yet the act of crossing no longer produced the sense of progression that had defined it at the beginning. The field remained open, the boundaries remained visible, and the path remained unbroken, yet the relation between where he was and where he was going no longer held as something complete.

The change had not arrived in a way that could be marked, but it had begun, and the field no longer entirely agreed with itself as he continued across it.

The misalignment did not remain slight, and it did not resolve itself through continued movement, but extended into a condition in which the field no longer maintained a single, coherent relation between its surface and the space it occupied, so that what had first presented as a subtle inconsistency became a sustained divergence between where he stood and what the field indicated about that position. The ground beneath him remained firm, the openness unchanged, and the boundaries still visible, yet the correspondence between these elements no longer held as a unified structure, the field continuing to present itself while no longer agreeing with the movement that crossed it.

He continued forward, not because the alignment remained, but because the absence of alignment did not produce an alternative, the act of walking still available even as its meaning shifted. The distance ahead did not resolve into approach, and the far edge no longer appeared to move in relation to his position, remaining fixed in a way that suggested neither proximity nor removal, so that the act of moving toward it no longer produced measurable change. The field extended, but it no longer translated extension into progress.

The paths that had once crossed the field lost their directional function entirely, their faint lines still visible in places yet no longer corresponding to any clear orientation, some seeming to lead toward boundaries that did not align with where they appeared to end, others fading into the ground without reaching anything that could be recognized as an edge. He did not attempt to follow them, and their presence no longer reinforced his own movement, leaving him within a surface that could be crossed without confirming where it led.

The wind shifted again, no longer moving across the field in patterns that could be traced, but rising in small, irregular currents that altered direction without transition, the grass bending in multiple directions at once, not violently but without coherence, the motion visible yet not readable. The air carried no force that would interrupt his balance, yet it no longer corresponded to the space in a way that could be understood, the field holding movement within it without organizing that movement into pattern.

He slowed, not deliberately but because the relation between step and outcome no longer sustained itself, his body adjusting to a condition in which continued movement required attention that could not resolve what had changed. Each step landed with the same firmness as before, yet the placement no longer contributed to a sense of crossing, the surface receiving him without carrying him forward in the way it once had.

The boundaries of the field remained visible but no longer functioned as points of orientation, the tree line holding its shape without anchoring direction, the road remaining along the edge without confirming relation, and the rise ahead continuing to exist without drawing nearer. The elements that had once defined the field now existed without forming a system that could be used, their presence no longer translating into guidance.

He turned slightly, not to reverse direction but to test whether the relation between movement and position might be restored through alteration in alignment, yet the shift in orientation did not produce a different outcome, the field presenting the same condition regardless of the direction he faced. The ground remained consistent, the openness unchanged, and the boundaries still present, yet none of these produced variation in the result of movement.

He continued, though the act of continuing no longer carried purpose, the steps following one another without building toward anything, the distance beneath him accumulating without forming relation, and the field extending without resolving. The sense of being within a place began to separate from the act of moving through it, the openness no longer functioning as space that could be crossed, but as a condition that held him without reference to where he had been or where he intended to go.

The air thickened slightly, not in weight but in presence, as though the space itself no longer allowed for passage in the way it once had, the movement of his body no longer opening distance ahead of him but remaining contained within what already existed. The field did not resist him, yet it did not yield, the act of crossing replaced by the act of remaining within.

He looked again toward the far edge, not to confirm distance but to test whether the boundary still held relation to his position, yet the confirmation did not occur, the edge remaining visible without aligning with where he stood. The field had not changed in form, yet it no longer behaved as a field that could be crossed, and the structure that had once defined it had separated from the experience of moving within it.

He continued because stopping would not restore what had been lost, the movement sustained without expectation, the surface holding without guiding, the field extending without leading, and the condition settling into place not as a moment of realization but as a state that repeated itself with each step, confirming that the field no longer held a single, consistent form as he moved through it.

The field did not break, and it did not collapse into something that could be recognized as failure, but reached a point at which its surface, its boundaries, and the space it contained no longer formed a single system that could be used, so that the act of crossing it no longer functioned even while every visible element remained present and intact. The ground continued beneath him, the openness extended in every direction, and the edges remained visible, yet none of these could be relied upon to produce orientation, the field holding together in form while separating in function.

He continued walking because the act of walking still existed, though it no longer produced movement in the sense that had once defined it, the steps following one another without generating change, the distance beneath him accumulating without forming relation to anything beyond itself. The field received each step without translating it into progress, and the continuity of motion no longer corresponded to the continuity of space.

The boundaries no longer behaved as limits that defined the field, not disappearing but losing their capacity to anchor position, the tree line holding its shape without confirming direction, the road remaining at the edge without establishing relation, and the rise ahead persisting without drawing nearer or marking distance. These elements existed, but they no longer connected, each remaining present while no longer participating in a structure that could be followed.

He slowed until his movement approached stillness, not because the ground required caution, but because the absence of result altered the nature of motion itself, his body responding to a condition in which continuing no longer produced difference. When he stood without moving, the field did not change, and when he resumed, the same condition held, the distinction between stillness and movement no longer creating variation in his relation to the space around him.

The air held him in the same way the ground did, not resisting but not yielding, the space through which he moved no longer opening ahead of him but remaining constant, so that motion occurred within it without altering it. The field extended through that air without interruption, yet the extension did not carry him forward, and the sense of passage no longer formed through movement.

He turned fully this time, aligning himself in the opposite direction from which he had come, and began to walk back along the line he believed he had followed, yet the field did not respond to reversal any more than it had to continuation, the boundaries remaining where they had been, the openness unchanged, and the distance failing to resolve in either direction. The act of returning did not restore what had been lost, and the field did not reassemble into something that could be read.

He adjusted again, altering his path at an angle, then another, not searching but testing, the variations in direction producing no change in outcome, the surface beneath him remaining constant while the relation between movement and place remained absent. The field no longer responded to direction, and the act of choosing where to go no longer altered where he was.

The sense of position separated from the act of locating it, the field no longer offering a point within itself that could be held as fixed, so that even the idea of being somewhere within it began to lose meaning. The openness remained, yet it did not function as space that could be occupied in a way that distinguished one place from another, the continuity of the field no longer containing difference.

He stopped again, and the stopping did not clarify anything, the field remaining as it was, the boundaries still visible, the surface unchanged, yet none of these providing orientation, and the act of standing no longer offering a vantage from which the space could be understood. The field held him without locating him.

He resumed walking, not because walking would produce change, but because the absence of movement did not alter the condition, the steps continuing as an action without effect, the surface receiving him without carrying him, and the openness extending without leading. The field remained, and he remained within it, yet the relation between them no longer formed into something that could be used.

The realization did not arrive as a single moment, but as a condition that repeated itself without variation, each step confirming what the last had already suggested, that the field could no longer be crossed, that direction no longer functioned within it, and that movement no longer produced position. The structure of the field remained visible, but its capacity to hold meaning had been removed.

He continued because there was nothing else to do, the motion sustained without expectation, the field extending without resolution, and the space holding him within it without offering a way through.

The field remained open, its surface unbroken and its boundaries still visible from wherever he stood within it, and nothing within its appearance suggested that it had become unusable, yet the condition that had taken hold did not recede and the relation between ground, direction, and position did not restore itself through time or through continued movement, so that what had changed did not reverse and what had separated did not return to coherence.

He stood within it without attempting to locate himself, his body present on the surface that still held his weight, his orientation no longer determined by the edges that could be seen but not used, and the openness that had once allowed for crossing now functioning only as extension without passage, the field not denying him movement and not obstructing him in any visible way, yet no longer permitting movement to become transition so that the act of going did not produce the condition of arriving.

The boundaries remained where they had always been, the tree line forming a clear edge, the road tracing the side of the field, and the rise still visible toward the far boundary, yet none of these elements provided position in the way they once had, their presence no longer connecting to his location within the field so that seeing them did not mean that he could reach them and knowing where they were did not establish where he was.

He walked again, not toward any one point but within the space that remained available, his steps continuing because they could, the ground receiving each one without resistance, the surface unchanged, and the openness extending without interruption, yet the movement did not produce difference and the distance did not resolve, the act of crossing remaining absent even as the motion of walking continued.

The air held steady around him without signaling change, not carrying pressure that would indicate direction, and the light remained even across the field, illuminating everything without revealing anything new so that the space continued to present itself fully while withholding the capacity to be used, the field neither concealing itself nor distorting its form yet no longer functioning as something that could be understood through movement.

He turned again, not to find a way out but because the body continued to respond to the absence of orientation by attempting it, the change in direction producing no alteration in outcome, the surface beneath him remaining consistent, the boundaries still visible, and the relation between movement and place still absent, so that the act of turning no longer reoriented him and the field did not respond.

He slowed until his movement nearly ceased and then resumed without reason beyond continuation, the rhythm of his steps no longer connected to distance, the act of walking no longer producing relation, and the space holding him without change, the field remaining and his presence within it continuing even as the distinction between being somewhere and moving toward somewhere no longer held.

Time passed without measuring anything within the field, the duration of his movement not corresponding to distance covered or position reached, the sequence of steps continuing without accumulating into progress, the field extending without variation and the condition neither deepening nor lessening but holding and repeating itself without alteration.

He did not leave the field, not because it held him in place, but because leaving it required direction that could no longer be formed, and the openness that surrounded him did not provide an edge that could be reached through movement, the boundaries remaining visible yet no longer functioning as exits, their presence no longer connected to the act of reaching them.

He continued walking, not toward a destination but within the condition that had replaced it, the steps following one another without leading, the surface holding without guiding, and the openness extending without offering passage, the field remaining what it appeared to be and his presence within it continuing even as the relation between them no longer formed into something that could be used.

There were moments when he stopped entirely, standing within the open span without movement, and the absence of motion did not alter what held, the field remaining unchanged, the boundaries still visible, and the distance unresolved so that stillness did not restore orientation any more than movement had, the condition holding across both without variation.

He resumed again, not because resuming would change anything, but because the act of continuing had not ended, the motion persisting even when its purpose had not, the structure of walking remaining even as its function had been lost, and the field extending forward without leading anywhere beyond itself so that the field remained and he remained within it and the act of crossing did not occur.

PART V

The Ones Who Carry It Forward

STORY 14

The Anniversary

BEFORE THE DATE CARRIED weight that altered the way it was entered, it existed as part of a sequence that did not require attention, one day following another without distinction beyond what was assigned to it by ordinary use, the calendar marking its position without attaching significance that would extend beyond its place within the year, so that it arrived as other days arrived, contained within the structure of time that moved forward without interruption, and passed in the same way, leaving nothing behind that required return.

The date had once been marked, though not in a way that set it apart from others beyond the small recognition that accompanies repetition, the acknowledgment that a year had turned and that something remembered had occurred within that turning, the marking not altering the day itself and not interrupting the sequence in which it appeared, but introducing a point at which attention briefly rested before continuing, the passage of time recognized without being held.

He knew the date before he saw it, the awareness forming not through the act of checking but through the way it approached, the days leading toward it carrying a slight alteration that did not yet define itself as difference but did not remain entirely unchanged, and when the calendar confirmed what he already understood, the number present in its place, the month aligned with it, and the year extending beyond it as it always had, the recognition did not settle in the same way it had before.

The morning began without disruption, the sequence of actions aligning with what had come before, the routine intact, the movements carried out without interruption, yet the continuity did not fully hold, the act of beginning the day no longer separate from the knowledge of what it contained, the ordinary structure remaining visible while no longer absorbing what had come with the date.

He moved through the house in the same order as before, the rooms unchanged, the objects remaining in their places, and the surfaces holding what had been set upon them, yet the familiarity did not function in the same way, the repetition of movement no longer producing the same sense of continuity, the house not altering while his relation to it shifted slightly, not enough to be named but enough to be present within every movement.

The calendar remained where it had been, visible without requiring attention, yet he looked at it more than once, not to confirm the date but to remain within it, the number holding its place without change while the meaning attached to it did not remain fixed, the passage of years not removing the date and the repetition of its arrival not diminishing its presence, yet neither allowing it to remain exactly the same.

He stepped outside for a moment, not because the day required it, but because the space within the house did not contain the full extent of what had begun to form, the air outside carrying no difference in temperature or movement, the sky unchanged, and the street holding its usual quiet, so that nothing within the environment marked the date and nothing indicated that it should be treated differently, yet the absence of change did not restore the sense that the day was the same as any other.

The memory did not arrive all at once, and it did not present itself as a single image or event that could be held and examined, but as a condition that existed alongside what was present, not replacing it but altering the way it was experienced, the date not bringing the past forward in a form that could be revisited, but not allowing it to remain separate either, the distance between then and now narrowing without closing.

He returned inside and continued with the tasks that the day required, the sequence moving forward without interruption, yet the movement through it did not carry the same sense of completion, each action following the last without resolving into a day that could be contained within itself, the structure remaining while the containment did not.

The clock marked the passage of time as it always had, the hours moving forward, the intervals consistent, and the measure unchanged, yet the sense of duration altered slightly, the day not passing in the same way, the movement through it not aligning fully with the measurement of it, the time remaining correct while the experience of it did not match.

He sat for a moment without intending to remain there, his attention not fixed on anything specific, the space around him holding its shape, the objects remaining where they were, and the light entering through the window at the same angle it had before, yet the stillness did not settle into rest, the pause not resolving into completion as the date remained where it was within the day and the day did not pass through it in the same way it had before.

The day did not continue alongside the date in the way it had before, and the sequence of hours no longer held independent of what the date contained, but began to reorganize itself around it, the ordinary structure of time remaining visible while no longer functioning as a separate frame, so that each movement within the day carried some relation to what had occurred within it in another year, the present not replaced but no longer isolated.

He moved through the next set of tasks with the same outward consistency, the actions performed in the same order and the objects used in the same way, yet the movement through them did not remain contained within their function, each action extending beyond itself not in thought but in condition, the day no longer holding as a series of discrete moments but as a single span that did not fully separate what was happening from what had happened.

The memory did not form into a sequence that could be followed, and it did not present itself as something he could choose to enter or avoid, but began to exist within the day in a way that altered its structure without interrupting it, the past not intruding but aligning, the events of the present no longer proceeding independently of what had once occurred on the same date, the distance between them continuing to narrow without becoming a single point.

He sat at the table and placed his hands against the surface, not resting in a way that produced stillness but maintaining contact as if the position itself might stabilize what did not hold, the objects before him unchanged, the room consistent, and the light entering as it always had, yet the space no longer contained the moment in the way it had before, the present extending beyond itself into something that could not be located within the room.

The clock continued to move forward, the measure of time uninterrupted and the intervals consistent, yet the relation between one hour and the next did not align with the experience of passing through them, the progression remaining accurate while the sense of movement through it altered, the day no longer advancing in a way that could be tracked through sequence alone.

He stood and moved again, not because the movement would resolve anything but because remaining still did not alter the condition, the actions continuing without pause and the structure of the day maintained, yet the containment within that structure continuing to fail, the present moment no longer closing behind him as he moved through it but remaining open and connected to what had already occurred within the same date in another year.

The memory did not sharpen into clarity and did not recede into distance, but held its position within the day without resolving into either presence or absence, the events of that earlier time not replayed but not absent either, the condition of them carried forward without needing to be reconstructed, the awareness of them existing without requiring recall.

He moved through another room and paused without intending to, the transition from one space to another not producing separation, the house no longer holding distinct areas in the way it had before, each room connected not only by physical structure but by the continuity of the day itself, the date extending through all of it without allowing one space to remain untouched by it.

Outside, the light shifted slightly, the progression of the day continuing in its ordinary pattern, yet the change in light did not register as movement toward evening but as variation within a day that did not pass in the same way, the sense of duration remaining inconsistent with what could be measured, the hours continuing without resolving into completion.

He looked again at the calendar, not to confirm the date but to remain aligned with it, the number unchanged and the page holding its place, yet the act of looking did not fix the day in place and did not restore separation between what was present and what had been carried into it, the date remaining constant while the meaning attached to it continued to shift within the experience of it.

He continued through the day without attempting to correct what had altered, the movement sustained not by expectation but by continuation, the actions proceeding in the same order while no longer producing the same sense of sequence, so that the day did not pass in the way it once had but remained held in place, its structure intact while its movement through time no longer completing itself.

The day did not continue as a sequence that could hold both what was occurring and what had already occurred within it, and the balance that had allowed the present to move forward alongside the date began to fail, so that the past did not simply align with the day but began to determine it, the structure of time no longer holding as something that progressed independently of what had taken place within the same date in another year. The hours still moved, the clock continued, and the light shifted, yet the relation between these movements and the experience of the day no longer held, the present no longer containing the past but yielding to it.

He continued with the actions that remained available to him, not because they carried meaning but because they could still be performed, the body moving through motions that had not changed while the context within which they occurred no longer held stable. The tasks did not fail, and the objects responded as they always had, yet the completion of each action did not produce separation from what had preceded it, the day no longer dividing into parts that could be left behind.

The memory did not arrive as recollection, and it did not require effort to maintain, but existed within the day as something that no longer remained distinct from what was occurring, the events of that earlier time not reassembled but present in a way that altered the present without replacing it. The distance between then and now did not collapse into a single point, but it no longer held as distance, the separation between them no longer functioning as boundary.

He stood at the window and looked out without searching for anything, the street beyond unchanged, the movement of the day continuing in the same pattern it always had, yet the scene did not remain separate from what the date contained, the present no longer forming its own layer of experience, but existing within a condition that included what had already occurred. The view did not alter, yet it did not remain entirely present.

The clock marked another hour, the sound consistent, the movement of the hands uninterrupted, yet the passage did not register as progression, the interval not closing behind him as something completed, but remaining open, connected to what had already been carried into the day. The measure of time continued, but the experience of it no longer aligned with sequence.

He moved again, not because movement would restore the structure that had begun to fail, but because remaining still did not prevent its continuation, the actions continuing in their ordinary form while no longer producing ordinary result. The house held its shape, the rooms remained distinct, and the objects remained in place, yet the separation between spaces no longer contained experience, each part of the house now holding the same condition, the date extending through all of it without interruption.

The memory no longer appeared alongside the present but within it, not replacing what he saw or did, but altering the way those things existed, so that the act of standing, moving, or looking did not occur independently of what had happened within the same date. The past did not interrupt, and it did not demand attention, yet it no longer allowed the present to exist without it.

He sat again, not in rest but in continuation, the position not resolving into stillness, the act of sitting not separating him from the day, the space around him unchanged, yet the condition holding within it without variation. The objects remained where they were, the light continued to move, and the sound of the clock persisted, yet none of these established the day as something distinct from what it had become.

Outside, the progression toward evening continued in measurable ways, the light lowering, the shadows lengthening, yet these changes did not produce the sense that the day was moving toward completion, the passage of time continuing without resolving into ending. The structure remained, but the outcome did not follow.

He did not attempt to separate the present from what had entered it, and he did not attempt to return the day to what it had been, because the condition did not respond to effort, and the sequence did not restore itself through intention. The date held, and the day remained within it, the movement of time continuing without producing distance from what had occurred.

He continued through the hours that remained, not because they would carry him beyond the date, but because they would not, the day holding its position without passing through him, the present no longer moving ahead of what had been brought into it, and the structure of time continuing without reestablishing the separation it had once maintained.

The day did not recover its sequence, and the structure that had once allowed time to move forward while containing what had occurred within it did not return, but reached a point at which the present no longer held independent form, the hours continuing to pass without producing distance from what had already taken place, so that the day did not progress beyond the date but remained within it, the movement of time no longer carrying him away from what it contained.

He continued to move because movement still existed, though it no longer separated one moment from another, the actions available to him remaining unchanged while their completion did not produce closure, the sequence of tasks no longer forming a progression that could be followed from beginning to end. The day extended, but it did not unfold, and the passage through it did not create the sense of having moved beyond any part of it.

The memory did not intensify, and it did not diminish, but held in the same position within the day without altering its form, the events of that earlier time not becoming clearer or more distant, yet no longer existing as something apart from what was occurring. The past did not intrude upon the present, and it did not recede from it, but remained within it, the two no longer existing as separate conditions.

He stood again within the house, his position unchanged in relation to the space around him, yet the space no longer functioning as something that could contain the moment, the rooms holding their structure while no longer holding experience within boundaries that could be distinguished. The walls remained, the doors remained, and the objects remained in place, yet the separation between spaces did not produce separation in what was carried through them.

The clock continued, its movement precise, the intervals consistent, the sound marking time without interruption, yet the marking did not produce progression, the hours no longer forming a sequence that moved toward completion, but existing within the same condition that had already taken hold. The measure of time remained accurate, but it no longer described what the day had become.

He attempted to mark the passage in a small way, adjusting something on the table, aligning an object that did not require alignment, the gesture not intended to change the day but to confirm that change could still occur within it, yet the action completed itself without altering anything beyond its own moment, the condition remaining unchanged before and after it, the movement not extending into the structure of the day.

He moved toward the door and opened it, stepping outside again, the air unchanged, the street continuing in its ordinary pattern, the light further along in its descent, yet none of these elements established that the day was moving toward its end, the progression visible but not functioning in the way it had before. The environment did not contradict the passage of time, yet it did not restore it either.

He stood there for a moment, not waiting, not observing, but remaining within the position that the day allowed, the present not forming into something that could be distinguished from what had already occurred, the date holding without movement, the hours continuing without separation.

He returned inside, not because the outside differed, but because movement between spaces still occurred even when the meaning of that movement had altered, the transition not producing change in the condition, the house receiving him in the same way the field of the day held him, without distinction between where he was and what the day contained.

The memory remained without shifting, and the day remained without resolving, the two no longer forming separate layers of experience, but existing within the same structure that did not progress. The past did not end, and the present did not begin anew, the continuity between them holding without variation.

He continued through what remained of the day, not because it would end, but because it had not, the movement sustained without expectation of completion, the hours continuing to pass without producing distance from what had occurred. The date held, and the day did not move beyond it, the structure of time remaining visible while no longer functioning as something that could be completed.

The day did not end in the way that days had ended before, and the movement toward evening did not resolve into a separation between what had been held within it and what would follow, but continued without producing distance, the light lowering, the shadows lengthening, and the hours passing while the date remained fixed within them, so that the conclusion of the day did not carry him beyond it but left him within the same condition that had formed when it began.

He remained within the house as the light changed, the rooms taking on the altered tones of evening, the objects still in place, the surfaces unchanged, yet the transition from day to night did not produce closure, the passage from one state to another not completing itself, but extending the same condition into a different form, the structure of time continuing to move while the experience of it did not align with that movement, the day not passing out of itself but continuing to hold what it contained.

The memory did not recede as the light diminished, and it did not deepen into something more defined, but remained in the same position it had held throughout the day, neither intensifying nor fading, the events of that earlier time no longer separate from what was occurring, yet not replacing it, the two continuing within the same unbroken condition, so that the past did not withdraw into distance and the present did not establish itself independently, leaving both held within a structure that did not divide them.

He moved through the house again, not because movement would change the condition, but because it had not ended, the act of walking from one room to another still available even as it no longer produced transition in the way it once had, the spaces remaining distinct in form yet no longer containing separate moments, each room holding the same condition, the date extending through all of it without interruption or variation.

Outside, the street grew quieter, the ordinary signs of evening continuing as lights appeared in windows and the movement of others diminished, yet these changes did not signal the closing of the day in the way they once had, the progression visible but not functioning as conclusion, the world beyond him moving forward while the day he remained within did not release him into that movement.

He sat again, not in rest but in continuation, the position not resolving into stillness, the act of sitting not separating him from the condition that held, the objects before him unchanged, the clock continuing its steady movement, the sound marking intervals that did not accumulate into completion, so that the passage of time remained measurable while no longer corresponding to an ending.

He did not attempt to mark the close of the day, and he did not attempt to separate himself from what it contained, because the condition did not respond to such efforts and the structure of time did not restore itself through intention, the date remaining where it was, not moving forward, not receding, and the hours that followed not carrying it away.

The light diminished further and the house entered the dimness that would ordinarily indicate the arrival of night, yet the transition did not complete itself, the absence of light not producing the sense that the day had ended but extending the same condition into another form, the boundary between day and night no longer functioning as a division between what had been held and what would come after.

He remained within that dimness, the space around him unchanged in structure, the objects still present, the walls still enclosing, yet the experience of being within it not separated from what the day had carried, the condition continuing without alteration, the date neither passing into memory nor settling into something that could be left behind.

At one point he stood without intending to, his body rising without decision, his position shifting within the same space, the movement not producing change, the condition holding across both stillness and motion, the act of continuing remaining available even as it no longer produced progression.

He did not leave the day, not because it held him in place, but because it did not release him, the difference subtle but absolute, the condition not imposed but unbroken, the date remaining where it was while he remained within it, neither advancing nor returning, but continuing without transition.

The day did not end.

And he remained.

STORY 15

The Question That Remains

THE QUESTION DID NOT arrive as a sentence, and it did not form in language at the moment it first appeared, but entered as a condition that altered the structure through which everything else had been understood, a quiet disruption that did not interrupt thought so much as make its continuation uncertain. It did not demand to be asked, and it did not announce itself as something new, yet once present, it remained, not moving forward into articulation and not receding into absence, but holding in a way that prevented the return of what had existed before it.

He recognized the change not by what had been added, but by what no longer aligned, the familiar sequence of interpretation no longer completing itself in the way it had, the connection between event and meaning no longer holding without effort, the world continuing to present itself in the same forms, the same objects, the same movements, the same language offered in explanation, yet something within the process of receiving those things no longer settled, the conclusion no longer forming at the end of the sequence as it once had.

It was not confusion, because the facts remained intact and the structure of what had occurred did not dissolve or distort, the sequence still able to be described, the details still able to be recalled, and the explanations still able to be repeated in the same words that had been used before, so that nothing had been lost in the sense of information. What had shifted was the capacity of those facts to arrive at completion, the ability of explanation to close upon itself and produce an end point that held, the final movement of meaning no longer sealing what had been understood.

He did not speak the question, and he did not attempt to define it, because the act of forming it into language did not seem to correspond to what it was, and any attempt to reduce it to a sentence produced something that did not carry the weight of the condition itself. It remained instead as a presence beneath thought, shaping the way each conclusion formed and then failed to hold, the answer arriving and then remaining incomplete even as it finished its own structure.

The day continued around him with its ordinary movement, the tasks available to him unchanged, the expectations of others remaining intact, the systems within which he moved still functioning as they had before, yet the question remained within all of it, not interrupting action but altering the way action resolved. He completed what was required, and the completion did not produce the same sense of having reached an end, the action closing without closing anything beyond itself, the sequence intact but its meaning unsealed.

He noticed it most clearly in conversation, when others spoke with certainty, offering explanations that had once aligned with his own understanding, their language structured in ways that led from premise to conclusion without hesitation. He could follow what they said, recognize the validity of the steps they took, and agree with the sequence as it unfolded, yet when the conclusion arrived, it did not settle, the final statement remaining open in a way that was not visible to them, the answer holding its form while failing to hold its weight.

He did not interrupt or challenge what was said, because the language remained accurate within its own structure and he did not have an alternative that could replace it, so the question did not provide answers, generate new conclusions, or offer correction. It simply remained, preventing the closure that had once followed explanation, leaving the end of each conversation slightly incomplete even when no one else recognized that anything was missing.

He found that he could repeat the same explanations himself, drawing from the same sources, using the same language, and constructing the same sequences that led others to resolution, and when he did, the words held, the structure remained intact, and the conclusion arrived as it always had. Yet within him it did not settle, the final statement remaining provisional even as it was spoken with the same tone of certainty that others used, the completion intact in form but not in effect.

The question did not oppose belief and did not replace it, but existed alongside it, altering the way belief completed itself without removing its structure, so that he continued to say what he had always said and continued to affirm what had always been affirmed without withdrawing from the language that had formed him. Yet the completion of that language no longer carried the same finality, the statements remaining open at their edges, the certainty no longer closing the space that followed them.

He did not experience this as doubt in the usual sense, because doubt suggested the possibility of resolution through further clarification, the expectation that the question would eventually be answered if pursued with enough precision, while what remained did not move toward resolution or suggest that an answer existed elsewhere. It did not direct him toward a different conclusion but remained where it was, within the structure of what had already been understood, preventing that structure from closing.

He attempted at times to move past it by returning to the forms that had once held, repeating them with greater attention, examining them more closely, testing their coherence, and confirming their internal consistency, yet each time the process completed itself, the same condition remained, the conclusion forming and then failing to hold in the same way, the question present without articulation, without expansion, and without resolution.

It was not constant in intensity and did not press upon him with equal force at every moment, because there were times when it receded slightly, when the movement of the day carried him through sequences that required enough attention to reduce its presence, and when action itself provided a temporary alignment that resembled what had existed before. Yet even in those moments it did not disappear, remaining beneath the surface, unchanged, waiting without intention and present without demand.

At other times it became more visible, not because it increased, but because the conditions around him allowed it to be seen more clearly, when the absence of distraction left space for it to hold without interruption, and when the completion of a task or the end of a conversation revealed the gap that followed, the place where conclusion no longer settled.

He did not name it, not because it could not be named, but because naming it would suggest that it had taken a form it had not yet taken, that it had become something defined and something that could be addressed directly, when in fact it remained prior to that stage, existing before language and shaping it without being contained by it.

It remained, and because it remained, everything else continued differently, even when it appeared the same.

The question did not move him away from what he had been doing, and it did not require him to stop, yet it altered the way each action completed itself, so that what once carried a sense of conclusion now ended without closing, the task finished while something within it remained unresolved. He continued to move through the same patterns, to meet the same expectations, and to inhabit the same roles that had structured his days, but the internal alignment that had once accompanied those movements no longer held in the same way.

He found that the disruption was most visible in moments that had previously required no reflection, when the ordinary completion of something small would have passed without notice, such as placing an object where it belonged or responding to a question that did not carry weight beyond its immediate context. These actions still occurred, and they occurred correctly, yet the sense of having completed them did not settle, the conclusion of the action no longer extending into a sense of completion beyond itself.

He could not identify a single point at which the change had begun, because it had not entered as an event that could be located, but as a condition that became visible only after it had already taken hold. There was no moment to return to, no instance to examine that would explain its origin, and no interruption in the sequence of events that could be marked as its beginning. The question did not arise from a single cause, and it did not attach itself to a single memory, but existed within the structure of understanding itself, altering the way that structure functioned without replacing it.

He noticed that others continued without this interruption, their movements aligned with the same patterns that had once governed him, their conclusions arriving with the same certainty that had previously defined his own. They spoke of what had happened in ways that preserved coherence, offering explanations that accounted for the sequence of events, and their language did not falter at the point of conclusion. For them, the structure still held. For him, it no longer closed.

He did not withdraw from them, and he did not isolate himself from the shared space of conversation and action, but he became aware of a separation that did not depend on distance, a difference in how the same events resolved within each of them. He could participate fully in what was being said, respond in ways that aligned with expectation, and carry the conversation forward without disruption, yet beneath that participation the question remained, preventing the same sense of completion from forming within him.

The question did not accuse, and it did not demand an answer, yet it altered the weight of what had already been said, so that statements which once settled into certainty now remained slightly open, their edges no longer sealed by the language that contained them. He did not reject those statements, and he did not replace them, but he could no longer experience them as final, the conclusion no longer functioning as an end point.

He attempted to approach the question indirectly, not by naming it, but by examining the structure around it, testing whether the disruption lay in something adjacent to it rather than within it itself. He revisited the sequence of events, not to change them, but to confirm their accuracy, retracing the order in which things had occurred, ensuring that nothing had been overlooked or misremembered. The sequence remained intact. The facts did not shift. The structure of what had happened did not reveal any inconsistency that could account for the change in how it was now understood.

He examined the explanations that had been offered, the frameworks through which others had interpreted what had taken place, and he found that they remained internally consistent, the logic within them holding as it always had. There was no error that could be corrected, no missing element that could be supplied to restore completion. The explanations worked, and yet they did not resolve what remained.

The question did not invalidate those explanations, but it prevented them from reaching the point where they could be considered complete. It did not oppose them, and it did not replace them with alternatives, but remained alongside them, creating a condition in which multiple understandings could exist without any one of them closing the space entirely. The presence of the question did not produce contradiction, but it did produce incompletion.

He found that the more precisely he attempted to define the edges of what he knew, the more clearly the question remained beyond those edges, not because it lay outside the scope of understanding, but because it existed within it in a way that could not be reduced to the same terms. It did not expand when examined, and it did not become clearer, yet it did not diminish either. It held its position regardless of the effort applied to it.

At times, he considered whether the question might eventually resolve itself through time, whether the continued passage of days might restore the alignment that had been altered, allowing the structure of understanding to close once more. Yet as time passed, the condition did not change, and the question did not move toward resolution. It remained as it had been, unaffected by duration, not deepening into something more complex, but not fading into something less present.

He recognized that what had changed was not temporary, and that the expectation of resolution might not apply to what remained. The question did not behave as problems did, and it did not invite the same process through which problems were addressed. It did not move toward an answer, and it did not suggest that one existed elsewhere. It simply remained, altering the way all other answers were received.

He continued to move within the structures that had formed his life, and those structures continued to function, allowing him to act, to speak, and to participate in the world as he had before. Yet within all of it, the question remained, not interrupting the movement itself, but preventing it from closing, so that each completed action, each spoken conclusion, and each resolved sequence carried within it a space that did not resolve, a remainder that could not be removed.

He did not resist it, because resistance implied that it could be opposed, and he did not accept it in the sense of resolution, because it did not offer itself as something that could be settled. Instead, he continued within it, the question present without form, shaping what followed without being answered, and remaining as the condition within which everything else now occurred.

The question began to reveal itself more clearly not by changing its form, but by exposing the limits of the structures that had once contained understanding, the places where explanation had previously completed itself now holding without closure. It did not expand into something larger, and it did not become more complex, but it became more visible through contrast, through the repeated experience of reaching the end of a thought and finding that the end no longer held.

He noticed this most distinctly when he returned to the account of what had happened, not in search of revision, but in the act of recounting it as it had been, the sequence of events still available to him in full, the order intact, the details precise enough to be placed within their proper positions. He could describe where he had been, what had occurred, and how it had unfolded, and the description would hold, the narrative complete in form, yet when it reached its conclusion, it did not resolve into something finished, the ending no longer functioning as an end.

Others received his account without hesitation, their responses aligning with what was expected, their understanding forming in ways that allowed them to move from the telling into conclusion, and from conclusion intocontinuation. They acknowledged what had occurred, recognized its weight, and incorporated it into the broader structure of meaning that allowed them to proceed. For them, the narrative completed itself. For him, it did not.

He found that the act of telling did not change the condition of the question, and that repetition did not move it toward resolution. Each time the sequence was spoken, it arrived at the same point and stopped in the same way, the final statement holding without closing, the narrative complete but not resolved. The question remained at that point, not as something added to the story, but as the absence of completion within it.

He began to recognize that the question did not belong to the content of what had happened, but to the structure through which what had happened was understood. It did not ask why in the sense of seeking cause, and it did not ask how in the sense of seekingmechanism. It did not direct itself toward the elements that could be analyzed or explained. Instead, it remained at the level of meaning itself, altering the way meaning concluded without altering the facts that gave rise to it.

He attempted, at times, to approach it by reframing what had occurred, by considering whether a different perspective might produce a different resolution, whether the same events viewed through another lens might close in a way that the original framing did not. He considered alternative explanations, alternative emphases, and alternative interpretations, and each of them held within its own structure, each capable of being articulated and defended. Yet none of them closed the space that remained, the question persisting regardless of the frame through which the events were viewed.

The question did not demand an answer in the form of explanation, and it did not respond to the multiplication of perspectives. It did not shift when approached from different angles, and it did not yield when examined more closely. It remained in the same position, not because it resisted inquiry, but because it did not participate in the same process.

It did not function as a problem to be solved, and therefore the methods that applied to problems did not apply to it.

He found that this altered not only how he understood what had already happened, but how he approached what was happening now, the present no longer forming into conclusions in the same way, the outcomes of events remaining slightly open even when they resolved in practical terms. A conversation could end, a decision could be made, an action could be completed, and yet the sense of finality that had once accompanied those endpoints no longer formed. The structure remained intact, but the closure did not.

He did not speak of this difference often, because the language available to describe it tended to convert it into something else, something that resembled doubt or uncertainty or confusion, none of which accurately described what remained. He could say that things no longer felt complete, but that would suggest an emotional response rather than a structural change. He could say that answers no longer satisfied, but that would imply dissatisfaction rather than the absence of closure. The question did not fit within the available categories, and so he allowed it to remain unnamed.

There were moments when the presence of the question became more pronounced, not because it increased, but because the conditions around him made its presence unavoidable, when the completion of something that once would have resolved now stopped at its edge, the absence of closure more visible because it contrasted with what had previously been expected. In those moments, the difference was not subtle. It was clear that something fundamental had shifted, that the process through which meaning formed had been altered in a way that did not revert.

At other times, the difference was less apparent, the movement of the day carrying him through sequences that required attention enough to reduce the visibility of what remained, the question still present but not at the forefront of awareness. In those moments, it might have appeared that the structure had returned, that the alignment had been restored, yet when the sequence reached its end, the same condition appeared, the closure not forming, the question remaining.

He began to understand that the question did not come and go, but that his awareness of it shifted depending on the conditions around him, the presence constant, the visibility variable. It did not depend on circumstance, and it did not respond to effort. It remained regardless of what he did, shaping the way everything else concluded without being altered by those conclusions.

He did not attempt to remove it, because removal implied that it did not belong, and he did not attempt to resolve it, because resolution implied that it could be completed. Instead, he continued within it, allowing it to remain where it was, the question present without form, without answer, and without end, defining the space within which everything else now occurred.

The question did not remain confined to reflection, and it did not limit itself to moments of recall or interpretation, but extended into action, altering the way decisions formed and the way outcomes were understood, so that even when he moved forward, the movement did not produce the same sense of arrival. He continued to choose, to act, and to respond within the demands placed upon him, yet the completion of those choices no longer settled into certainty, the result holding in place without closing the process that had led to it.

He found that the shift was most evident not in large decisions, where uncertainty might be expected, but in those that had once required little consideration, the small determinations that had previously resolved themselves within the context of routine. He could decide what to do, carry it out, and observe its result, and all of this would occur without disruption, yet the sense that the decision had fully resolved the situation did not follow, the action completing itself while the meaning of that completion remained open.

This did not prevent him from acting, and it did not paralyze him in the face of choice, because the structures that governed action still held, the criteria still available, the outcomes still observable, and the consequences still real, allowing him to move forward within those structures even as the question remained beneath that movement. It did not oppose the action, but prevented its finality, so that something remained unclosed even after the decision had been carried through.

He noticed that this altered the way he experienced responsibility, not in the sense of reducing it, but in the way it extended beyond what could be completed, the awareness that no action fully resolved the condition from which it arose. He could do what was required, meet the demands placed upon him, and fulfill the expectations that defined his role, yet the completion of those actions did not produce the same sense of having done enough, the boundary between action and its adequacy no longer clearly defined.

He did not interpret this as failure, because the actions themselves remained intact, the outcomes measurable and, in many cases, sufficient within the terms that had always governed them, so that what had changed was not the effectiveness of what he did, but the sense that effectiveness equated to completion. The alignment between doing and finishing no longer held in the same way, and the result could be achieved while the question still remained.

He found that this extended into his understanding of others as well, the actions of those around him no longer resolving into the same judgments they once had, the tendency to assess, to conclude, and to settle upon an interpretation of what someone had done now interrupted by the same condition. He could see what had been done, understand the reasons behind it, and recognize its effects, yet the final judgment did not hold, the conclusion remaining open in a way that prevented it from fully closing.

This did not lead him to suspend judgment entirely, because the need to respond, to act in relation to others, and to make determinations did not disappear, and he continued to engage, to respond, and to participate in the structures that required those responses. Yet within each of them the question remained, altering the sense that any judgment could fully resolve what it addressed, so that even clarity did not produce finality.

He became aware that the question did not remove meaning, but that it altered its boundaries, preventing it from sealing itself in the way it once had, so that meaning still formed, conclusions still emerged, and understanding still developed, yet each of these remained slightly open. Their edges were no longer fixed, and the finality that had once accompanied them was replaced by a condition that allowed for continuation without closure.

He did not resist this, because resistance implied that the previous condition could be restored through effort, and he did not attempt to return to what had been, because the change did not present itself as something reversible. Instead, he continued within the altered structure, allowing decisions to be made, actions to be completed, and responses to be given, while recognizing that none of these would produce the same sense of completion they once had.

There were moments when the absence of closure became more pronounced, when the completion of something significant did not bring with it the expected sense of resolution, and when an outcome that would once have marked an end now remained open, the continuation extending beyond what had been achieved. In those moments, the question was not more present, but more visible, the difference between what had been and what now was more clearly defined.

At other times, the difference was less apparent, the movement of activity providing enough structure to carry him through without drawing attention to what remained, the question still present but not at the forefront of awareness, yet even in those moments the condition did not change. When the sequence reached its end, the same absence of closure appeared, the same unsealed conclusion remaining where resolution had once been expected.

He began to understand that the question was not something that could be answered, because it did not ask in the way that questions normally did, and that it did not point toward an answer, because it did not exist within the same framework as answers. It remained instead as a condition that redefined what it meant for something to be complete, altering the expectation that completion would close what had been opened.

He continued to act within this condition, not because he had resolved it, but because it did not prevent action, the structures that governed movement still present, the expectations still requiring response, and the world still demanding participation. Yet within all of it, the question remained, shaping the way each action concluded without ever concluding itself, its presence extending into everything he did without becoming something that could be finished, so that he moved forward without arrival and continued without closure within what remained open.

The question did not resolve into an answer, and it did not withdraw in the face of time, but remained as the day moved toward its close, extending through the transition from light into dimness without altering its form. The movement toward evening did not bring with it the expectation of conclusion, and the structure that had once allowed the end of a day to carry what had occurred into distance no longer functioned in that way, the passage of hours continuing while the condition remained unchanged.

He stayed within the same spaces as the light shifted, the rooms taking on the subdued tones of evening, the outlines of objects softening without disappearing, and the familiar environment holding its shape even as its meaning no longer aligned in the same way. The change in light did not produce separation between what had been experienced and what followed, and the day did not release what it contained into memory, but held it within the same continuous structure.

The question remained present without increasing and without diminishing, its position unchanged even as the conditions around it altered, so that the transition from one part of the day to another did not move him beyond it. The past did not recede into distance, and the present did not establish itself independently, leaving both within the same field of experience, the boundaries between them no longer functioning as they once had.

He moved through the house without intention to change anything, his actions continuing because they had not ended, the movement from one room to another still available even as it no longer produced transition in meaning. The structure of space remained intact, yet the sense that movement between spaces marked progression did not hold, each location carrying the same condition, each position within it shaped by what remained unresolved.

Outside, the environment shifted in ways that would ordinarily signal the closing of the day, the light lowering across the street, the sounds diminishing, and the visible activity of others reducing as evening took hold, yet these changes did not establish conclusion. The world continued to move forward in its own pattern, but that movement did not carry him beyond what had already formed, leaving him within a day that did not end in the way it once had.

He did not attempt to bring the day to a close, because the condition did not respond to such effort and the expectation of closure no longer aligned with what remained. He could observe the progression of time, hear it marked in the steady movement of the clock, and see it in the change of light, yet these markers did not produce an end point that held, the measure of time continuing without corresponding to completion.

The question did not become clearer in the quiet, and it did not recede into the background as activity diminished, but remained as it had been throughout the day, neither demanding attention nor allowing itself to be set aside. It existed beneath the surface of thought, shaping the way each moment concluded without becoming the object of that thought, present without form and without resolution.

He sat for a time, not to rest but because sitting remained available, the act not separating him from the condition but occurring within it, the stillness not producing clarity and not diminishing what remained. The space around him held its structure, the objects unchanged, the boundaries intact, yet none of it contained the experience in a way that allowed it to close.

He recognized that the question was not something that would be answered at the end of the day and that the expectation of resolution through time did not apply to what it was, because it did not move toward completion and did not exist within a sequence that led to conclusion. It remained instead as the condition within which time now moved, the passage of hours occurring without carrying it forward or leaving it behind.

He did not attempt to define it, because definition would suggest that it had taken a form that could be addressed, and he did not attempt to resolve it, because resolution would imply that it could be completed. Instead, he allowed it to remain where it was, recognizing that it had become part of the structure through which everything else was now experienced, not separate from it but embedded within it.

The light diminished further, and the house entered the quiet that accompanies the end of the day, yet the quiet did not bring with it the sense of conclusion that had once followed, the transition into night not marking an end but extending the same condition into another form. The boundary between day and night no longer functioned as a division between what had been held and what would follow, and the day did not pass into something that could be left behind.

He remained within that condition, not because he chose to remain but because there was no movement that would carry him beyond it, the question continuing without change, the structure of time continuing without resolution. The day did not end in the way it once had, and what remained did not diminish as it passed, so that the condition persisted without alteration while he continued within it, not arriving and not concluding, but moving forward inside what remained open.

STORY 16

The One Who Stays Silent

SILENCE DID NOT BEGIN as an absence of speech, and it did not enter as a decision to withhold, but formed gradually as the space between what could be said and what could be completed widened, the words still available while their ability to arrive at meaning no longer held in the same way. He continued to speak at first, responding as expected, offering the language that had always been used in moments that required it, yet something within that language did not settle, the statements reaching their end without carrying what they once had.

The change was not immediately visible to others, because the words themselves remained intact, their structure unchanged, their tone consistent with what had been spoken before, and their placement within conversation still aligned with expectation, so that he answered questions, participated in exchanges, and fulfilled the role that speech required even as something beneath that continuity had altered. The connection between what was said and what it completed no longer held, and the difference existed without outward disruption.

He noticed it first not in what he said, but in what followed after, in the moment when language had once resolved the need for it and brought something to rest, a point that no longer arrived in the same way. Conversations continued or ended without the sense that anything had been concluded, the words remaining as structure without sealing what they contained, the expected closure absent even when the exchange itself appeared complete.

He did not stop speaking immediately, because silence had not yet formed as an alternative and because the expectation to speak remained present, the patterns of interaction still requiring response. He continued to answer, to explain, and to contribute, yet each time the same condition appeared, the words completing themselves while leaving something unclosed, the conclusion of speech no longer aligning with the completion of meaning.

He became aware that the repetition of language did not restore what had shifted, that speaking more clearly or more precisely did not resolve the gap that remained, and that the effort to refine what he said only revealed more clearly that the structure itself had changed. The words could be made more exact, the explanation more thorough, and the tone more measured, yet the result did not differ in the way that mattered, the end of speech still failing to close what it once had.

Others did not recognize the change at first, because the outward form of communication remained intact and the absence that had begun to form did not yet present itself as silence. They continued to ask, to respond, and to engage, and he continued to meet those engagements, the exchange proceeding without visible disruption even as its internal completion no longer occurred.

The shift became more apparent over time, not because he spoke less in measurable terms, but because the weight of what he said began to alter, the words carrying less of what had once been assumed within them and the statements no longer functioning as endpoints. He could say what was required, yet the saying did not complete what it addressed, leaving something open that had once been closed by speech itself.

He began to pause more frequently, not out of hesitation, but because the moment that had once followed speech no longer formed automatically, the transition from speaking to completion no longer occurring without attention. These pauses were not yet silence, but they marked its approach, the space between words lengthening slightly, the continuation of speech no longer immediate because the structure that had once carried it forward without interruption no longer held.

He did not attempt to fill those pauses, because the effort to do so did not resolve the condition that produced them and the addition of more language did not restore what had been lost. Instead, he allowed the pauses to remain, not as an intentional withholding, but as a recognition that speech no longer carried the same function it once had, and that continuation alone would not produce completion.

The conversations around him continued, others speaking with the same patterns of certainty and completion that had once defined his own speech, their words arriving at conclusions that held for them and their language still functioning as a means of resolution. He could follow what theysaid, understand the structure of their meaning, and respond when required, yet within him the same gap remained, the completion not forming even when the conversation itself reached its end.

He found that listening did not resolve what speaking could not, that the reception of language carried the same condition as its expression, the words of others also arriving without closing the space they described. The conversation could proceed, information could be exchanged, and understanding could be reached in a functional sense, yet the deeper sense of completion that had once accompanied those exchanges did not return, the structure holding without sealing.

The silence began there, not as the absence of words, but as the absence of closure within them, the condition in which speech no longer completed what it once had and in which the continuation of language did not alter that fact. It formed gradually, not through refusal, but through recognition, the awareness that speaking no longer produced the same result even when it remained necessary.

He did not decide to stop speaking, because the process did not present itself as a choice and the structures that required speech remained in place, continuing to call for response. He answered when he was addressed, spoke when it was necessary, and participated when participation was expected, yet the internal alignment that had once accompanied those actions no longer held, the words functioning without completing.

Over time, the distinction between speaking and remaining quiet began to shift, not because one replaced the other, but because both existed within the same condition, the presence or absence of words no longer determining whether something had been resolved. He could speak and leave something open, and he could remain quiet and leave it equally open, the difference between the two no longer corresponding to completion.

The silence did not isolate him and did not remove him from the structures within which he continued to live, but it altered the way he occupied them, the absence of closure within speech extending into his presence among others. He remained engaged, present, and responsive, yet something within that engagement no longer concluded, the interaction continuing without sealing what it contained.

He did not name this change, because naming it would suggest that it could be defined in the same terms as what had preceded it, and the language available did not hold the difference without altering it. Instead, he allowed it to remain as it was, the silence forming within speech, not replacing it, but existing within it as the condition that had taken hold.

He continued to speak, and he continued without completing what speaking once had, the words present, the structure intact, and the closure no longer forming within them.

The silence did not replace speech, and it did not require the absence of words in order to be present, but extended within the act of speaking itself, altering the way language functioned so that what had once resolved through expression now remained open even as it was said. He continued to participate in the structures that required him to speak, responding when addressed, offering explanations when asked, and contributing to conversations in ways that aligned with expectation, yet within each exchange the same condition remained, the words completing their form without completing their work.

He found that this became more visible in interactions that required more than simple response, when others sought not only information but assurance, and when the act of speaking was expected to carry weight beyond its immediate content. In those moments, language had once provided more than description, serving as a means of stabilizing what was uncertain and of bringing something unsettled into a form that could be held, yet now the words still arrived, the sentences still formed, and the explanations still followed their expected structure, while the effect did not hold in the same way, the assurance not settling into place even as it was offered.

He could recognize the expectation in the way others listened, in the slight pause that followed his words as if waiting for something within them to complete itself, the moment when what had been said would ordinarily become enough. That moment no longer arrived, and although others often moved forward as if it had, he remained aware that something had not closed, the exchange continuing while its resolution did not.

He did not attempt to compensate by speaking more, because the addition of language did not produce the completion that had been lost, and he did not withdraw entirely, because the structures within which he lived still required participation. Instead, he continued within the altered condition, allowing speech to occur while recognizing that it no longer functioned as it once had, the presence of words no longer equating to the presence of closure.

There were times when he noticed that his responses had become more measured, not in the sense of caution, but in the sense of recognizing the limits of what speech could accomplish, the awareness that no arrangement of words would fully resolve what they addressed. He did not reduce what he said, and he did not obscure it, but he no longer expected it to carry beyond its own form, the statement ending where it ended without extending into completion.

Others began gradually to sense the change, not as something they could name, but as a difference in the way conversations settled, the slight absence of finality in exchanges that would once have concluded more fully. Some responded by continuing to speak, adding to what had been said in an attempt to reach the closure that no longer arrived, extending the conversation beyond its natural end in search of something that would complete it, while others allowed the exchange to end as it was, moving forward without addressing the absence directly, the incompletion present but unspoken.

He remained within both kinds of interaction, responding when conversation continued and allowing it to end when it did, the condition unchanged regardless of how the exchange proceeded. The silence did not depend on whether words were present, and it did not diminish when more was said, remaining instead as the structure within which speech now occurred, shaping it without being altered by it.

He noticed that this extended into how he understood what others said as well, the reception of language no longer producing the same sense of completion that had once followed it, even when the speaker reached a clear conclusion. He could follow the logic, understand the intention, and recognize the validity of what was being expressed, yet the same openness remained, the final statement not closing the space it described.

This did not lead him to dismiss what was said, because the content remained intact, the meaning still accessible, and the function of communication still operative within its necessary bounds, allowing him to act on what he heard, respond appropriately, and continue within the exchange. Yet beneath that functionality the absence of closure remained, the silence present within the words themselves and not removed by their use.

He became aware that the difference did not lie in communication as a system, but in the relationship between language and completion, the assumption that speaking could bring something to rest no longer holding in the same way. Language still described, still conveyed, and still connected, yet it no longer concluded, the expectation that words would finish what they began no longer supported by the structure within which they occurred.

At times he considered whether silence in the more conventional sense, the absence of speech, might align more closely with what had changed, whether choosing not to speak might reflect more accurately the condition that had formed. Yet he found that silence in that sense did not resolve what remained any more than speech did, because the condition did not depend on the presence or absence of words, and he could remain quiet and still encounter the same incompletion, the same openness that speech no longer closed.

He did not adopt silence as a position, because it did not function as an alternative, and he did not abandon speech, because it remained necessary within the structures of his life. Instead, he moved between the two without assigning resolution to either, recognizing that both existed within the same altered condition, the difference between them no longer corresponding to completion and neither producing what had once been expected.

The silence that had formed was not something he could enter or leave, and it did not mark a boundary between one state and another, but existed as the environment within which both speech and quiet occurred, the condition that held regardless of what he did. It did not isolate him from others, and it did not remove him from participation, but it altered the way participation resolved, the end of each exchange no longer sealing what it contained.

He continued to speak when speech was required, and he continued to listen when others spoke, the exchange of language proceeding as it always had, yet within that exchange the silence remained, not as absence, but as the lack of closure that speech no longer provided. The words moved, the conversations continued, and the structures held, yet something within them did not complete, and the presence of that incompletion defined the condition within which he remained.

He did not attempt to correct this, because correction implied that something had gone wrong, and what had changed did not present itself as an error. It presented itself as a condition that did not respond to adjustment or repair and did not revert through effort, remaining as it was while shaping the way language functioned without being altered by that function.

He remained within it, speaking and listening without arriving at completion, the words present, the structure intact, and the silence continuing within them as what no longer closed.

The silence did not remain confined to speech, and it did not limit itself to conversation, but extended into presence itself, altering the way he occupied space among others so that even when he was fully engaged, something within that engagement no longer resolved. He continued to be where he was expected to be, to stand within rooms, to sit among others, to move through shared environments in ways that aligned with the patterns that had always governed those movements, yet the completion that had once accompanied presence did not form in the same way, the act of being there no longer closing the space between himself and what surrounded him.

He found that this difference was not visible in outward behavior, because he remained attentive, responsive, and aligned with the expectations that defined his role, his posture unchanged, his gestures consistent, and his participation intact, yet internally the same condition held, the sense that presence did not complete itself, that being there did not fully arrive. The environment received him, and he responded within it, yet the alignment between presence and completion no longer held.

Others did not immediately recognize this change, because the external markers of engagement remained, the signs that indicated attention and participation still visible, and the structure of interaction continuing without disruption. He could listen, respond, and contribute, and the exchange would proceed as it always had, yet beneath that continuity the silence remained, the absence of closure extending beyond words into the very act of being present.

He noticed this most clearly in moments that once required no reflection, when simply standing within a space had been enough to establish belonging, when the act of being there completed itself without question. Now, the same act occurred, yet the completion did not follow, the presence holding without settling, the space not fully closing around him in the way it once had.

This did not produce separation in the conventional sense, because he did not withdraw, and he did not become absent from the environments he inhabited. He remained within them, visible, engaged, and responsive, yet something within that presence did not resolve, the alignment between himself and the space remaining slightly open, the sense of being fully situated no longer forming.

He found that movement did not change this condition, because shifting from one place to another did not produce arrival in the way it once had, the transition occurring without the corresponding sense of having reached a new position in any final way. He could enter a room, take his place within it, and engage with those present, yet the act of arrival did not complete itself, the position held without closing.

At times, he considered whether this might be corrected through greater attention, whether by focusing more deliberately on where he was and what he was doing he might restore the alignment that had been lost, yet the effort did not produce the desired effect. Attention increased awareness, but it did not produce completion, and the presence remained open even under deliberate focus.

He observed that others did not experience this in the same way, their movements still producing arrival, their presence still completing itself within the spaces they occupied, their engagement resolving into the sense of being fully there. He could see it in the way they settled into positions, in the ease with which they moved from one environment to another, and in the way their interactions reached points of rest that held without effort.

He did not attempt to imitate this, because the difference did not lie in behavior, and the outward forms of presence could not restore what had shifted within it. He could align his actions with theirs, follow the same patterns, and occupy the same spaces in the same ways, yet the internal condition remained unchanged, the absence of closure persisting regardless of how precisely he mirrored what had once come naturally.

The silence extended through all of this, not as withdrawal, but as the absence of completion within presence, the condition in which being there no longer fully resolved into itself. It did not isolate him, because he remained connected, and it did not remove him from participation, because he continued to engage, yet it altered the way that engagement concluded, the end of each interaction and each movement no longer sealing what it contained.

He began to recognize that the silence did not belong to any single aspect of experience, but moved across all of it, from speech into listening, from action into presence, and from movement into stillness, the same condition appearing regardless of what he did. It did not depend on context, and it did not respond to change, remaining consistent across all environments and interactions.

He did not resist it, because resistance implied that it could be opposed, and he did not attempt to resolve it, because resolution implied that it could be completed. Instead, he continued within it, allowing himself to remain present, to move, and to engage, while recognizing that none of these would produce the sense of closure that had once accompanied them.

There were moments when the difference became more visible, when the absence of completion contrasted sharply with what had once been expected, when the act of being present in a particular space did not carry the sense of belonging or arrival that had once defined it. In those moments, the silence was not louder, but clearer, its presence more easily recognized because it stood against the memory of what had been.

At other times, the difference receded slightly, not because it diminished, but because the conditions around him required enough attention to reduce its visibility, the movement of activity carrying him forward without drawing attention to what remained. Yet even in those moments, the condition did not change, and when the activity paused, the same openness remained.

He did not name this, because naming it would place it within a framework that suggested it could be understood in the same way as what had preceded it, and the language available did not hold the difference without altering it. Instead, he allowed it to remain as it was, the silence extending through presence, not replacing it, but existing within it as the condition that had taken hold.

He remained where he was, moving and standing and engaging within the spaces that continued to receive him, yet within all of it the silence remained, the absence of closure within presence itself, so that he was there without fully arriving, present without fully completing what presence once had.

The silence did not remain contained within speech or presence, but extended into memory itself, altering the way what had already occurred could be held, so that recollection no longer resolved into something that could be fully retained. He could remember, and he did remember, the sequence of events, the structure of what had taken place, and the details that defined it, yet the act of remembering no longer brought those elements into a form that felt complete. The memory held its content, but it did not settle, the recall arriving without closing.

He found that this difference did not lie in the accuracy of what he remembered, because the events remained clear, their order intact, and their details available to him without distortion, yet the completion that had once followed recollection did not occur. He could bring the past into the present through memory, and he could describe it if required, yet the act of doing so did not produce the sense that what had been recalled had reached an endpoint, the memory remaining open even as it was fully formed.

He noticed that this altered the way he returned to specific moments, the recollection no longer functioning as something that could be revisited and then set aside, but as something that remained present without resolving. He could enter into a memory, move through it, and arrive at its end, yet the exit from it did not occur in the same way, the boundary between remembering and continuing no longer clearly defined, so that the past did not release him once it had been recalled and the present did not fully reassert itself afterward.

This did not result in confusion between past and present, because he remained aware of where he was and when he was, yet the distinction did not carry the same functional clarity, the separation between what had been and what was now no longer producing closure. The memory existed within the present without being absorbed by it, and the present continued without fully containing it, leaving both in a shared condition that did not resolve.

He found that repetition did not alter this condition, because returning to the same memory multiple times did not bring it closer to resolution and did not allow it to settle into something that could be completed. Each time it was recalled, it held in the same way, the beginning accessible, the sequence intact, and the end present, yet the completion absent, the structure of the memory intact while its closure did not form.

He observed that others did not experience memory in this way, their recollections still arriving at points of rest, their accounts of the past forming into narratives that could be told and then left behind, the act of remembering producing a kind of completion that allowed them to move forward. He could recognize this in the way they spoke, in the way their memories resolved into statements that held without continuing beyond themselves.

He could participate in those exchanges, offer his own account, and align with the structure of narrative that others used, yet within him the same condition remained, the telling not resolving the memory and the conclusion of the account not sealing what it contained. The narrative could be completed in form, yet it did not complete the experience it described, leaving something open that could not be closed through repetition or refinement.

He did not attempt to alter his memory or to reshape it in ways that might produce closure, because the structure of what had occurred remained fixed and any effort to change it would not address the condition that had formed around it. The silence did not arise from the content of the memory, and it did not respond to adjustments in how that content was held, remaining instead as the absence of closure within the act of remembering itself.

At times, he considered whether the passage of time might restore the function that had been lost, whether distance from the events might allow memory to settle in the way it once had, yet as time passed, the condition did not change. The memory did not diminish, and it did not deepen, but remained as it was, unaffected by duration, the same openness present regardless of how far he moved from the moment in which it had occurred.

He recognized that the silence did not belong to the memory as such, but to the structure through which memory was experienced, the same condition that had altered speech and presence now extending into recollection, preventing it from completing itself. The past could be accessed, and it could be understood, yet it could not be closed, the act of remembering no longer carrying the function of resolution.

He continued to remember, not because it would lead to completion, but because it remained part of how he existed within the world, the past present within him in a way that could not be removed or resolved. He allowed the memory to remain as it was, neither attempting to resolve it nor to avoid it, recognizing that the condition did not respond to either approach and did not change through effort.

The silence remained within the memory, not as absence, but as the lack of closure that recollection no longer provided, the experience held without conclusion, the past present without being completed. It did not isolate him from what had been, and it did not distort it, but it altered the way it could be held, the memory no longer settling into a form that could be finished.

He carried it forward, not because it moved, but because he did, the memory remaining as it was while his position in relation to it continued to change, the silence within it unaltered by that movement. The act of remembering continued, and the completion did not follow, the structure intact, the content present, and the closure absent, so that what had been remained accessible without ever becoming finished within him.

The silence did not end, and it did not resolve into something that could be left behind, but remained as the day moved toward its close, extending through the transition from activity into stillness without altering its form. The structures that had once marked completion continued to appear, including the end of conversations, the finishing of tasks, and the movement from one part of the day into another, yet none of these produced the sense of conclusion that had once accompanied them, the sequence continuing while its closure did not form.

He remained within the same patterns that had always governed his life, the expectations unchanged, the actions still required, and the responses still given, yet the completion that had once followed these patterns no longer held. He could do what was necessary, fulfill what was asked, and move through each part of the day as it unfolded, yet beneath all of it the silence remained, the absence of closure extending through everything he did without interrupting it.

The difference did not isolate him from others, and it did not remove him from participation, because he continued to engage, to speak, to listen, and to act within the shared structures that defined his world. He was present, visible, and responsive, and those around him could not always see the change that had taken place, because the outward forms remained intact, yet within him the same condition held, the sense that nothing fully concluded and that each moment extended beyond itself without resolving.

He recognized that the silence was not something he could enter or leave, because it did not exist as a separate state, but as the condition within which all other states now occurred. It did not begin when he stopped speaking, and it did not end when he spoke again, and it did not depend on whether he was alone or among others, remaining constant while shaping everything without being shaped by it.

At times, the presence of the silence became more visible, not because it increased, but because the conditions around him allowed it to be seen more clearly, when the completion of something that would once have resolved now remained open, and when the expected sense of ending did not arrive. In those moments, the difference between what had been and what now was stood in clear contrast, the absence of closure no longer subtle and no longer easily overlooked.

At other times, the movement of the day carried him forward without drawing attention to what remained, the continuity of action providing enough structure to obscure the difference temporarily, yet even then the condition did not change. When the sequence reached its end, the same openness remained, the same absence of completion appearing where it once had not, confirming that the difference was not situational but structural.

He did not attempt to overcome it, because overcoming implied that it could be defeated or removed, and he did not attempt to resolve it, because resolution implied that it could be completed. Instead, he continued within it, allowing himself to move through the day as it required, while recognizing that the structure within which he moved had changed in a way that did not return to what it had been and did not yield to effort.

The silence did not diminish what remained of his life, and it did not remove meaning from what he did, but it altered the way meaning concluded, preventing it from sealing itself in the way it once had. He could still care, still act, still respond, and still participate, yet none of these reached a point of finality that held, the continuation extending beyond each completed moment without arriving at closure.

He understood that this was not a phase that would pass and not a condition that would resolve with time, because time had already continued without altering it, the days moving forward while the silence remained unchanged. It did not deepen, and it did not lessen, but held steady as a constant presence within the shifting conditions of his life, unaffected by duration and unmoved by progression.

He remained within it without naming it, because naming it would suggest that it could be defined and contained, and the language available did not hold what it was without altering it. It existed before language and continued beyond it, shaping the way language functioned without being fully expressed within it, present without form and without resolution.

The day moved toward its end, the light diminishing and the environment settling into the quiet that follows activity, yet the transition did not produce closure, and the movement into night did not mark an ending. The structures of time continued, but their function had changed, the passage from one moment to the next no longer carrying the sense of completion that had once defined it, leaving continuity without conclusion.

He did not leave the day in the way he once had, because it did not release him, and he did not carry it forward as something completed, because it had not concluded. Instead, he remained within the continuity that now defined his experience, the silence extending through both what had been and what followed, the condition unchanged as time continued and as movement persisted without resolution.

He remained not apart and not withdrawn, but fully within a life that no longer closed, a life that continued without finality and without completion, and within that life the silence stayed, not as absence, but as what no longer allowed anything to fully end.

Conclusion

Living After

THE STORIES IN THIS book do not end in the way stories are expected to end. There is no final movement that gathers what has happened and resolves it into something complete, no moment in which what was broken is restored to its original form, and no point at which the past is placed behind those who have lived through it. What remains instead is continuation, a life carried forward under conditions that have been altered in ways that do not reverse and do not fully integrate into what came before.

To live after is not simply to survive. Survival marks the fact of continuation, the body remaining where it might not have remained, the life extending beyond what might have ended. Living after, however, describes something more complex, a condition in which continuation does not restore coherence and does not return a person to the structure of meaning that once held. What has been experienced does not remain contained within memory as something completed, but continues to shape perception, action, and understanding in ways that do not resolve.

The individuals in these stories do not fail to move forward. They do move forward, and they do so with consistency, with effort, and often with care for others that remains intact even when their own sense of coherence has shifted. They return to homes, or to what remains of them. They rebuild structures. They enter conversations. They take on responsibilities. They participate in the shared life around them. Nothing in these actions is diminished. Yet within them, something does not close.

Moral injury, as it appears in these lives, does not always present as visible rupture. It does not always announce itself through breakdown or withdrawal. Often it exists as a quiet alteration in the way the world is held, a change in the relationship between action and meaning, between what is done and what can be made of what has been done. The injury does not lie only in what was lost, or even in what was endured, but in what could not be prevented, in what had to be chosen under conditions that did not allow for a whole outcome, or in what remained unresolved when no further action was possible.

There are moments in these stories when something decisive occurs, a hand that slips, a door that does not open, a line that does not reach, a name that remains on a list, a voice that does not answer. These moments are not always dramatic in themselves. Often they are quiet, contained within the flow of events, unnoticed by anyone not directly involved. Yet they become the point around which everything that follows is organized, not because they explain what has happened, but because they cannot be fully absorbed into understanding.

Living after means carrying such moments without completing them. It means continuing in a world that still functions, still requires participation, still offers structure and expectation, while knowing that something within that structure no longer holds in the same way. It means acting without the assurance that action will resolve what it once resolved, and speaking without the certainty that words will fully contain what has been experienced.

This does not mean that nothing remains. Care remains. Responsibility remains. Relationship remains. Even meaning remains, though it may no longer take the form it once did. People continue to act on behalf of one another. They continue to respond to need. They continue to show up in the spaces where life requires them. The presence of moral injury does not erase these capacities. It alters the ground on which they are exercised.

In some lives, the alteration is subtle, appearing only in certain moments, surfacing when a sound, a gesture, or a circumstance brings the past into the present in a way that cannot be set aside. In others, it is more constant, shaping the way each day is entered and carried. In all cases, it resists completion. It does not yield to time alone, and it does not resolve through explanation.

What, then, does it mean to live well after such experiences? The stories in this book do not offer a single answer, and they do not attempt to construct one. Instead, they show forms of endurance that do not depend on resolution. They show individuals who continue without requiring that what has happened be made whole. They show a kind of faithfulness that is not grounded in certainty, but in continuation itself.

There is a tendency to look for restoration that returns a person to who they were before, to imagine healing as a form of restoration that closes the distance between past and present. These stories suggest a different possibility, one in which the distance remains, and life continues within it. What is sought is not a return, but a way of remaining human within conditions that do not fully allow for wholeness.

Living after, then, is not defined by the removal of what has been carried, but by the capacity to continue carrying it without losing the ability to act, to care, and to remain present. It is not a resolution, and it does not produce one. It is a form of life that persists where closure does not.

These stories end without ending because the lives within them do the same. They move forward, not toward a point of completion, but within a continuity that remains open. The reader is not asked to resolve them, nor to supply what is missing. The task is simply to witness what remains when resolution does not come, and to recognize that what remains is still life, still action, still presence.

To live after is to remain.

Not unchanged.

Not completed.

But still here.

APPENDIX

Bearing What Remains

Recognizing and Responding to Moral Injury Among Survivors

THIS APPENDIX IS NOT a guide to resolution. It does not offer a sequence that leads from injury to repair, nor does it assume that what has been experienced can be brought to closure through the right set of interventions. Instead, it is meant to help those who accompany survivors—caregivers, responders, clergy, clinicians, and communities—recognize the presence of moral injury and respond in ways that do not deepen it.

Moral injury among survivors often goes unnoticed because it does not always appear as distress in the usual forms. It may not present as acute crisis, visible breakdown, or immediate dysfunction. Survivors may continue to function, to care for others, to rebuild, and to participate in the life around them. What has changed lies beneath these actions, in the relationship between what has been lived and what can be made of it.

To recognize moral injury is not to diagnose it in a clinical sense, but to perceive when a person is carrying something that does not resolve, something that cannot be integrated into a story that makes sense of it. It is to notice when the question is no longer "What happened?" but "How do I live with what cannot be undone?"

I. RECOGNIZING MORAL INJURY IN SURVIVORS

Moral injury often emerges in quiet ways. It does not always declare itself. The following patterns are not exhaustive, nor are they definitive, but they may indicate that a survivor is carrying unresolved moral weight.

1. Persistence Without Resolution

The survivor continues to function, often at a high level, yet certain moments remain open, returning without diminishing over time. These are not intrusive memories in the usual sense, but points of experience that do not settle into the past.

2. Altered Relationship to Choice

The survivor may speak of decisions made under pressure, but not in terms of regret alone. Instead, there is often a recognition that no available option would have been whole. The injury lies not in choosing wrongly, but in being required to choose within an impossible frame.

3. Language That Does Not Hold

When describing what occurred, the survivor may begin to speak and then stop, not because the memory is unclear, but because language fails to contain it. Phrases may trail off, repeat, or remain deliberately incomplete.

4. Continued Orientation Toward Others

Unlike some forms of trauma that draw attention inward, moral injury often retains an outward focus. Survivors may remain deeply concerned about others—those lost, those left behind, or those affected by decisions made. This concern persists even when no further action is possible.

5. Absence of Closure

Even when external circumstances have stabilized—recovery completed, homes rebuilt, lives resumed—the survivor may not experience a sense of ending. Events remain present in a way that does not align with the passage of time.

6. Embodied Recall

The injury may surface not through thought, but through the body: a hesitation at a doorway, a tightening of the hand, a reaction to sound or space that reflects a moment that did not resolve. These are not always dramatic. Often they are subtle, but consistent.

II. WHAT DOES NOT HELP

In the presence of moral injury, certain well-intentioned responses can unintentionally deepen the harm. These responses attempt to resolve what cannot be resolved or to restore what cannot be returned.

1. Forcing Meaning

Statements that attempt to assign purpose or reason to what occurred—"Everything happens for a reason," or "Something good will come from this"—can invalidate the survivor's experience. Moral injury often involves events that resist such framing.

2. Offering Premature Closure

Encouraging the survivor to "move on," "find peace," or "let it go" imposes an expectation that the experience can be completed. This can create additional strain when the survivor cannot meet that expectation.

3. Overemphasis on Choice

Focusing on what the survivor "could have done differently" misunderstands the nature of moral injury. In many cases, the available choices were all insufficient. The injury lies in the structure of the situation, not simply in the decision made.

4. Reframing Toward Positivity

Attempts to redirect attention toward gratitude, resilience, or growth may be appropriate in some contexts, but when used to bypass unresolved moral weight, they can feel dismissive. These elements may emerge over time, but they cannot be imposed.

5. Treating Silence as Absence

When a survivor does not speak about what occurred, it should not be assumed that the experience has been integrated or resolved. Silence may reflect the limits of language rather than the absence of impact.

III. WHAT HELPS

Responding to moral injury does not require solving it. It requires the capacity to remain present to what does not resolve and to support the survivor in continuing within that condition.

1. Bearing Witness Without Resolution

To listen without attempting to complete the story is one of the most important forms of care. This means allowing the survivor to speak in fragments, to leave things unfinished, and to return to the same point without pushing toward conclusion.

2. Honoring the Reality of the Moment

When survivors describe what they faced, it is often helpful to acknowledge the constraints they were under. Statements such as, "There may not have been a way to make that whole," can validate the structure of the experience without assigning blame or absolution.

3. Allowing Complexity to Remain

Moral injury often holds multiple truths at once: care and loss, action and limitation, presence and absence. Supporting survivors means allowing these to coexist without forcing them into a single interpretation.

4. Supporting Continued Agency

While the past cannot be changed, the survivor's capacity to act in the present remains. Encouraging engagement in meaningful action—not as repair, but as continuation—can help sustain a sense of agency without requiring resolution.

5. Recognizing Embodied Experience

Attending to physical responses—hesitation, tension, altered movement—can provide insight into how the injury is carried. These moments can be acknowledged gently, without interpretation, allowing the survivor to notice them without needing to explain them.

6. Remaining Present Over Time

Moral injury does not resolve quickly, and often does not resolve at all. Consistent presence over time, rather than brief intervention, is essential. The goal is not to move the survivor through a process, but to accompany them as they continue.

IV. QUESTIONS FOR REFLECTION AND CARE

These questions are not meant to produce answers, but to open space for reflection. They can be used by caregivers or offered to survivors, depending on context and readiness.

- What remains from that moment that does not settle?
- What did the situation ask of you that could not be fully given?
- Where do you notice the experience now—in thought, in memory, in the body?

- What continues, even though that moment did not resolve?
- What does it mean for you to keep living with this present?

These questions should be held lightly. They are invitations, not requirements.

V. FOR CAREGIVERS AND RESPONDERS

Those who accompany survivors may also encounter moral weight in the process. Witnessing what cannot be resolved, holding stories that do not close, and remaining present without being able to change what has occurred can create its own form of strain.

It is important to recognize that:

- You are not responsible for resolving what cannot be resolved.
- Your presence matters even when it does not produce change.
- Remaining with someone in what does not close is a form of care.
- You may also need spaces where your own experience can be held.

Moral injury is not only carried by those who directly experience the event. It can extend to those who stand alongside them.

VI. CLOSING PERSPECTIVE

To bear what remains is not to fix it. It is not to transform it into something else, or to carry it toward a resolution that may never come. It is to remain in relationship to it without turning away, and to support others in doing the same.

Survivors do not need to be made whole in order to continue living. They do not need their experiences to be resolved in order to act, to care, or to remain present in the world. What they need most is often not an answer, but a witness—someone who can remain with them in what does not close.

This appendix offers no final instruction because none can be given. It offers instead a way of seeing and a way of staying, grounded in the recognition that some things are not repaired, but are carried.

And still, life continues.

Acknowledgements

THIS BOOK WAS NOT written in isolation, even though many of the stories move through spaces where isolation is deeply felt. It arises from years of listening—to survivors, to responders, to those who have lived through moments that did not resolve and have continued to live within what remained. The voices behind these stories are not reproduced directly, but their presence shapes every page. I am indebted to those who have trusted me with what could not be easily spoken, and who allowed me to remain with them in experiences that resist completion.

My work in disaster response and spiritual care has brought me alongside individuals and communities at points of profound disruption. Through organizations such as the American Red Cross, faith-based disaster networks, and local and national VOAD partners, I have witnessed both the strength and the cost of staying present in the midst of loss. I am grateful for colleagues who have carried this work with integrity, humility, and endurance, and who continue to model what it means to remain human when the conditions do not support it.

I also acknowledge the broader Moral Injury Project, within which this book finds its place. The ongoing work of naming, exploring, and responding to moral injury—particularly through my partnership with Wipf and Stock Publishers—has created the space for these stories to exist as part of a larger conversation. This volume stands alongside After the Disaster: Moral Injury, Dignity, and the Lives of Survivors, extending its concerns into narrative form. I am thankful for the opportunity to develop both the conceptual and the narrative dimensions of this work.

To those in pastoral care, counseling, emergency management, and community leadership who engage these realities daily: your work often unfolds without recognition and without resolution. You bear witness to what cannot be repaired and remain present where others might turn away. This book is, in part, an acknowledgment of that quiet and demanding labor.

I am especially grateful to those who have read, reflected, and responded to earlier drafts of this work and to related projects. Your insights have helped shape not only the clarity of the writing but the integrity of its approach, ensuring that these stories remain grounded in respect for those whose lives they echo.

Finally, I offer thanks to those closest to me, whose patience and support make sustained work like this possible. Writing about what does not resolve requires time, attention, and a willingness to remain in difficult spaces. Your presence has made that possible in ways that extend far beyond what can be named here.

Any shortcomings in this work are my own. The responsibility for how these stories are told rests with me. The lives that have informed them, however, carry a weight and dignity that exceed what any book can contain.

This book is offered in recognition of that.

About the Author

Rev. Gregory C. Smith, PhD, is a minister in the Presbyterian Church (USA) and a longtime leader in disaster spiritual care. For decades, his work has placed him alongside individuals and communities navigating the aftermath of crisis, where loss, disruption, and moral complexity converge. He has served in multiple leadership and training roles within national disaster response networks and is a board member of the Iowa Disaster Human Resources Council, contributing to the ongoing development of care practices for responders and survivors alike.

Dr. Smith is the author of numerous books exploring moral injury, faith, and the lived realities of those who serve and those who endure. His work with Wipf and Stock Publishers forms part of a broader Moral Injury Project, a sustained effort to examine how moral rupture shapes both personal and communal life. Titles in this body of work include What the Work Asks, After the Disaster, The Beatitudes After Betrayal, and Blessed Are the Broken, among others.

In addition to his writing, he develops training resources and field-based frameworks for disaster responders, clergy, and caregivers, with a particular focus on sustaining humanity in environments that resist resolution. His work bridges theology, lived experience, and narrative, offering both conceptual depth and practical insight.

He lives in the Midwest and continues to write, teach, and support those engaged in the demanding work of care in the aftermath of disaster.

www.ingramcontent.com/pod-product-compliance
Lightning Source LLC
LaVergne TN
LVHW052314200926
848481LV00002B/566
* 9 7 9 8 3 8 5 2 8 5 9 0 7 *